PRAISE FOR *SMARK*

'That old, moss-covered wall between sales and marketing in the brick-and-mortar world, which went right ahead and started growing in the online world as well, has been showing its age for a long time now. It's great to see that the wrecking balls are on-site, and they're clearing the way for the type of collaboration that is long overdue. Some of us shout about it, but Hughes, Gray and Whicher take action and provide some answers.' **Ted Rubin, CMO and advisory board member at Photofy, MC and host at Brand Innovators Summits and co-founder of Prevailing Path**

'An artful read that eloquently delivers truth about the digital transformation of sales, marketing and business that any reader can understand. The examples and detail presented provide an excellent understanding of how the worlds of sales and marketing work today and the changes that are continuing to occur. I definitely recommend it for any business person who wants to stay current on where digital is and where it is going moving forward.' **Robert Caruso, partner at fondalo.com and Engage2Connect.com**

'*Smarketing* is a must-read for marketers, managers and business innovators ready to succeed in times of fast change and disruption. Not only does the book explain the new rules of marketing and sales, but also how to implement a step-by-step Smarketing transformation able to overcome any challenges that might arise along the way. Easy to read and full of practical knowledge on every page, *Smarketing* is a book that belongs in your personal library.' **Jan Barbosa, Global Brand Ambassador at beBEE.com and 2016 Top 100 Onalytica Augmented Reality Influencer**

'There's never been a time when aligning sales and marketing has been more important. *Smarketing* not only explains why this is more important; it provides deep insights into how to create the alignment necessary for the success of sales and marketing and gaining a competitive advantage.' **Melonie Dodaro, bestselling author of *LinkedIn Unlocked* and *The LinkedIn Code***

'A company brand is built on the promises it makes and the experiences it deliver. Align these two and you can build a goldmine! Much of your team's experience is delivered through your customer-facing team members. That's why it's imperative to empower your team to build their personal brand in order to build your company brand in order to enable the connections and conversations necessary to scale the business. Tim Hughes is a master of social selling and social business and his new book delivers how to implement these ideas company-wide.' **Jon Ferrara, CEO, Nimble Inc**

'It's been recognized for a long time that sales and marketing functions need to be more aligned, but the idea of this has always been seen as a challenge. It's great that *Smarketing* outlines a way for those organizations that want to achieve better collaboration and results.' **Tiffani Bova, author of *Growth IQ: Get Smarter About the Choices that Will Make or Break Your Business***

'There's little doubt that the customer is at the centre of today's business world. In a globally interconnected marketplace customers don't distinguish marketing from sales or customer service. They expect to connect with you wherever they are and whenever they want without being shoved from pillar to post or having to repeat their story. Business needs to adjust structurally to this new reality.' **Dionne Lew, author of *The Social Executive*, principal consultant and CEO**

'Truly aligning forces and collaborating is a key quality for organizations that want to survive and ideally shape their future for the "age of the customer". Hughes has been a true thought and action leader in defining the blend of social selling over the last few years. Together with Whicher and Gray, this book redefines how sales and marketing need to be blended. A clear must-read!' **Johannes Ceh, keynote speaker, owner and consultant at Strategic Management Consulting, #ValueEnhancer**

'The way we buy is changing significantly and the sales and marketing world is struggling to keep up with it. Tim Hughes, Adam Gray and Hugo Whicher have put together the single most comprehensive guide on how you as a salesperson, marketer or business can leverage this change to your advantage. Not only a must-read book but a hugely valuable asset for everyone who buys it.' **Daniel Disney, founder and CEO of The Daily Sales**

'Educated and demanding buyers will no longer tolerate being bombarded with blanket messages from vendors. This means that sales and marketing departments are now being forced to step up and transform to match the new buying journey... a journey that focuses on buyer outcomes (not vendor revenues) throughout the entire customer life cycle. As Tim, Adam and Hugo have rightly pointed out in this great book, this realignment requires a big shift in focus for most businesses. With a recent research report stating that "only 3 per cent of buyers can fully trust both Sales and Marketing personnel" it's now time for these two outdated business functions to transform and refocus on the buyer.

This is a great book that hits the nail fairly on the head... sales and marketing alignment, followed by alignment with the new empowered buyer is not critical.' **Graham Hawkins, CEO and founder, SalesTribe**

'Sales and marketing will never be the same again. Tim shows why success requires a yin-yang design as we make the shift from siloed approach to account-based strategies.' **Ray Wang, principal analyst and founder, Constellation Research**

Smarketing

How to achieve competitive advantage through blended sales and marketing

Tim Hughes, Adam Gray and Hugo Whicher

KoganPage

First published in Great Britain and the United States in 2019 by Kogan Page Limited

2nd Floor, 45 Gee Street	c/o Martin P Hill Consulting	4737/23 Ansari Road
London EC1V 3RS	122 W 27th St, 10th Floor	Daryaganj
United Kingdom	New York NY 10001	New Delhi 110002
www.koganpage.com	USA	India

© Tim Hughes, Adam Gray, Hugo Whicher, 2019

The right of Tim Hughes, Adam Gray and Hugo Whicher to be identified as the authors of this work has been asserted by them in accordance with the Copyright, Designs and Patents Act 1988.

ISBN   978 0 7494 8358 6
E-ISBN   978 0 7494 8359 3

British Library Cataloguing-in-Publication Data

A CIP record for this book is available from the British Library.

Library of Congress Cataloging-in-Publication Data
Names: Hughes, Tim, 1965- author. | Gray, Adam (Business writer), author. | Whicher, Hugo, author.
Title: Smarketing : how to achieve competitive advantage through blended sales and marketing / Tim Hughes, Adam Gray and Hugo Whicher.
Description: London ; New York : Kogan Page, 2019. | Includes bibliographical references and index.
Identifiers: LCCN 2018030972 (print) | LCCN 2018031958 (ebook) | ISBN 9780749483593 (ebook) | ISBN 9780749483586 (pbk.)
Subjects: LCSH: Marketing. | Selling. | Technological innovations. | Digital media.
Classification: LCC HF5415 (ebook) | LCC HF5415 .H844 2019 (print) | DDC 658.8–dc23

Typeset by Integra Software Services, Pondicherry
Print production managed by Jellyfish
Printed and bound by CPI Group (UK) Ltd, Croydon, CR0 4YY

CONTENTS

ACKNOWLEDGEMENTS

Tim Hughes

First and foremost I want to thank my parents Marian and David for always believing in me. Their comfort and support have made a massive impact in my life inside and outside of the work environment. I've inherited my father's love of ice-cream and music and my mother's drive and ability to organize; just some of the attributes that got me here, sitting embarking on what is my second book. I also want to thank my partner, Julie, for encouraging me and then making sacrifices while I spend my time with 'writing days'. I tell her all the time she is my hero and she is. She is always there to listen, challenge and support. Finally, I need to thank my two writing partners. Both of them are a big inspiration both on this journey and in my life. Adam, and I are changing the world since we set up Digital Leadership Associates, transforming business. A true inspiration. Hugo always surprises me about his attention to detail to this subject matter. His clarity of purpose on this project has also been energizing. Hugo and Adam, I raise my glass. Finally, to both the Gray and Whicher families, who too have made sacrifices; I thank them for supporting my co-authors.

Adam Gray

I would like to dedicate my portions of this book to my family – my children Maddy and Max, who make me laugh and are a constant source of pride (and purpose), and my long-suffering wife Jo, who has been a support and inspiration through the trials and tribulations of being a 'business widow' and with the writing of this book. I also need to thank Hugo, my co-author, for his expertise and brilliance. Most of all though I need to thank my business partner Tim, who has been a friend, a mentor and a great support during the writing of the book and in my daily business life. We very strongly share a vision for our company Digital Leadership Associates about changing the world, but Tim's ability to execute on that vision (and in a smaller way, the vision for this book) is a rare gift and one that I am very reliant on.

... and thank you too for buying and reading this book.

Hugo Whicher

I want to thank all of my family for their support and putting up with me disappearing to my study on weekends. When I decided to take on this project and work with Tim and Adam I had no idea the time and dedication it would take to complete but have loved every minute of it. I wanted to particularly thank the ladies of my house, my wife Amanda and daughter Bella, for letting me take the time away from them and also being my sounding boards. Thanks to my mother as well for her help with the overall readability of the book. I also wanted to mention my colleagues at my company, who are a massive inspiration to me, and particularly my marketing mentor Emmanuel, who has instigated a lot of my thinking. Additionally, I wanted to thank Mark for his views on business that have also helped me to shape a vision of Smarketing: great inspiration. And finally, thanks to my co-authors, with their great ideas and energy in helping to brainstorm and complete this book, particularly Tim, who after approaching me has been a constant help and guide every step of the way.

ABOUT THE AUTHORS

Tim Hughes

Tim Hughes is universally recognized as one of the world's leading pioneers and exponents of social selling and is currently ranked as the number one most influential social selling person in the world.

He was responsible for a large-scale sales transformation within a multi-billion software company, where he helped transform 4,000 salespeople from selling on-premise solutions to selling Cloud/Software-as-a-Service.

An element of this was implementing social selling across the European organization, which is where he got the inspiration to write his first Kogan Page book, *Social Selling: Techniques to influence buyers and changemakers*. As well as being a bestseller, the book is now used in many universities around the world, as well as the Institute of Digital Marketing in the UK, as essential reading.

Tim is currently leading a number of sales transformation programmes in large B2B organizations. He is the co-founder and CEO of Digital Leadership Associates.

Adam Gray

Adam has spent all his life working in marketing, most of it digital marketing. Ten years ago he moved exclusively into social media.

Subsequently he was approached by Pearson to write the first internationally published book on social media for business: *Brilliant Social Media*. He often speaks on the global conference circuit and appears on the BBC News.

In addition, Adam spent three years as Head of Client Social Media EMEA (Europe, Middle East and Africa) for a large multi-billion software company, working with their biggest clients to help them understand how they could deploy social media within their businesses and helping them to create implementation strategies.

He is the co-founder and COO of Digital Leadership Associates.

Hugo Whicher

Hugo's career has exclusively concentrated on B2B marketing, with a particular focus on engaging senior business professionals with technology solutions. With experience spanning the traditional marketing mix, and more recently with an emphasis on digital and account-based marketing, Hugo's approach has always been based around effective collaboration with internal teams and stakeholders. His experience, including as the marketing lead for a CRM implementation, has given him an in-depth understanding of the ideal interaction between sales and marketing teams to facilitate business success.

During his tenure in marketing technology, he has covered all the different areas that a business needs to successfully utilize tech: from hardware, middleware and applications, to the people who deliver any technology solution. Working successfully to deliver marketing programmes for these areas has been the focus of his career in account-based marketing, but his role has also seen him deliver one of the largest technology conferences in the UK for a multinational technology business.

On his downtime, Hugo enjoys refining his martial arts skills or heading to the hills on his mountain bike.

Digital Leadership Associates (DLA)

Tim and Adam formed Digital Leadership Associates (DLA) (www.social-experts.net) in September 2016 with the purpose to change the world with social media.

They spotted that companies can make significant competitive advantage, incremental revenue gains and internal efficiency increases by deploying social media strategically.

This is not about 'posting on social media', but using social as a strategic tool from the C-suite downwards and across all departments: marketing, sales, human resources, supply chain etc.

Since launching, they have built a global company through their extensive experience of working in and on large corporate organizations and have a number of Tier 1 clients.

Not only do they truly understand the challenges of corporate inertia, they also understand how to navigate within the political environment of large organizations.

Their programmes are NOT based on telling organizations what the problem or the opportunity is, but on showing them how to grasp the opportunity as well as providing the change programme to support the changes in people and process.

Introduction

Change will not come if we wait for some other person or some other time. We are the ones we've been waiting for. We are the change that we seek.
BARACK OBAMA

Disruption is the new norm

In the modern business world there often seems to be a tension between what the market is doing, what the customers are doing and what the business is doing. Sometimes it's difficult to see which of the three is driving advances in the others. Companies can be innovators, followers or laggards. They can drive the market (like Apple have done), they can follow the market (like Samsung have done) or they can be laggards, holding on to 'the old ways' of doing things because they are comfortable and often profitable too (like most of the high street banks). Each has their own business objectives and models for behaving in a particular way.

Each course carries with it risks – different risks, but risks none-theless. The Apples of this world risk developing, manufacturing and marketing a product that nobody wants. The Samsungs risk reduced margins by, as their position of follower, not being able to command the same prices that the innovator can command. However, it is the finan-cial services 'laggard' companies that carry the greatest risk. Companies like these have by nature become unable to embrace change; even though they themselves were once the disruptors, they have become comfortable in their middle age and this is the biggest risk of all.

Kodak, Toys-R-Us, Borders, Blockbuster and countless other disrup-tive brands became set in their ways and themselves became disrupted.

Many of you who are reading this may remember vinyl records (LPs, EPs and 45s); they were something that each of us as authors grew up with. Then, after vinyl records, there were cassettes and compact discs (CDs). Owning music and the physical asset was paramount. Ironically, music was social. You would sit around the record player and pass around the record sleeve to your friends as you listened to Elton John's Greatest Hits.

When Sony first undertook research and development on the Walkman the feedback was, 'Why would I want to listen to music on the move; I can listen at home'. It was the launch of iTunes on 9 January 2001 that shook the world; this was the turning point where you could download tracks. There was then another shift in 2008 whereby you didn't even need to download music or own it, you would just stream it. Spotify was launched on 7 October 2008. These major leaps forward came about because of other enhancements in infrastructure, such as the iPhone, WiFi, etc. Apple have since announced the end of their LP download format and it has been reported in the press that they plan to end downloads completely in the future, moving to an all-streaming model. In fact, vinyl records, as a vintage and retro statement, are now outselling downloads.

The interesting thing about this is that the medium was disrupted – records became cassettes which became CDs (progressively more robust and convenient), then the idea of physical media fell prey to the 'virtual media' with digital downloads that the customer could own.

Figure 0.1   Music formats over time © Digital Leadership Associates

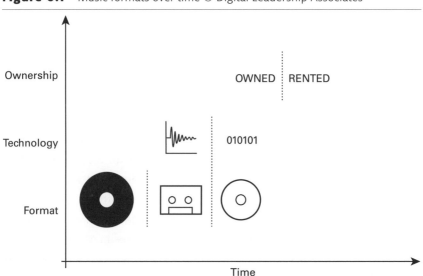

Then the actual ownership fell prey to the idea of 'renting music as you want it' so the disruption happened at every level of music interaction.

What we are seeing here is the norm being disrupted and then being disrupted again all in a matter of 10 years. We are seeing this level of disruption speeding up. In this chapter we will talk more about the disruption that is impacting our companies at the macro-economic level but also the disruption in sales and marketing.

Why are we writing this book?

It is worth saying from the outset that in this book we have sought to shake the sales and marketing world by its lapels (so to speak)! The 'business as usual' malaise that has paralysed both sales and marketing departments with a combination of 'that's good enough' thinking and a short-term view of what needs to be accomplished has to a certain extent backed sales and marketing departments into a corner. To escape from this position these departments will need to really double-down and think about some fairly fundamental changes in how they envisage themselves. It will also require significant action to be taken. Both sales and marketing need to stand up tall and see each other as a partner/equal and work much more closely together in a more joined-up fashion if they want to reverse this downward trend and get back to the glory days of the past.

We are unapologetic about this viewpoint, and whilst we are clearly speaking with passion about how we feel things need to change, this is not to say that we are simply having a 'rant' with this book, because we're not. Every point we make has been debated and discussed at length and everything has been researched both in terms of the problem and more importantly the solution. We hope that reading this will help you consider there are other ways that things can be done to maximize your business.

In our conversations with dozens of businesses (both in our working lives and as part of the background for this book) we have seen some organizations that have embraced the idea of Smarketing and, as a result, are thriving. But we have also seen organizations that are 'all at sea' and really don't know how to change how they operate in order to remain relevant to their customers and their prospects in the modern world.

We have included a significant interview in the book that shows in the real world how a large company has balanced the corporate inertia that can stifle change with the recognition that new technologies and new behaviours require new processes and of course new strategies. This company has made a great success of crafting a working regime for sales and marketing where they are intertwined in both a strategic and an operational way. Yes they still have different reporting lines and yes they have different budgets, but they are closely siamesed and clear that they have a shared goal of creating a great customer experience and generating revenue for the business. They plan together, they execute together and they are working towards a common goal. Marketing in this firm is *not* there to generate pipeline, it is there to generate *pipeline that closes* and there is a massive difference between the two. So, this example proves that sales and marketing can work differently together in the modern business world.

In every case with companies that we have interviewed, companies we have been part of and companies we have worked with there is no argument that things are very different today in terms of how organizations (and individuals) make their buying decisions and that this fundamental shift hasn't really been reflected in terms of how the sales and marketing machine within the corporate environment has moved to mirror those customer behaviours.

We acknowledge that corporate inertia, fear of change and 'we simply don't do things that way' thinking have been part of the problem, but there is also the very real issue that often people in sales and marketing (which, let's be honest, are pretty full-on jobs) simply haven't had the time to stand back and look at what they're doing and see that it somehow doesn't seem as connected to the customer as it once did.

So, with this book we have sought to give a clear signpost as to how organizations can embrace the idea of Smarketing and how they can be part of the transformation that needs to take place to be ready for the future. We are not, of course, saying that there's a Kodak moment going on, a moment where your products are outdated and no longer necessary in the modern world, because that's not a sales and marketing issue. What we are saying though is that there is a wider company issue about the relevance of the company's purpose in the modern world.

We are suggesting that sales and marketing are the first (and major) touchpoints when products and services are being selected, assessed and compared and that dovetailing how the company appears to how those decisions are now being made is vital for businesses today and in the future if they don't want to suffer the same fate as many big name businesses over the last couple of decades.

If you think this will never happen to your business because you're too big, too successful or you simply have too much brand recognition in the marketplace to fail, think again. As Capgemini Consulting pointed out, you are very clearly 'not safe', no matter how much your business appears to be a safe and secure 'institution'.

> @CapgeminiConsul *Since 2000, 52% of companies in the Fortune 500 have either gone bankrupt, been acquired or ceased to exist.* 10 May 2015 – 6.25 pm

The change that your company (don't worry, not just yours but almost every company) needs is significant, but you needn't be scared about this because you could view this as increased clarity in your department's purpose, or a new adventure, or a chance to change the world. One thing is for certain: in this game there is everything to play for as very few companies seem to be embracing the change (yet) and this means that for you and your company there is a great opportunity for first-mover advantage.

Whilst this might seem like wishful thinking, it isn't. We can be reasonably certain that the idea of working for a disruptive company like Amazon, Airbnb, Snapchat or Facebook is exciting and whilst this is certainly the case, disruption comes in many forms, internal and external. When we think of disruption we often focus on what the company does as the disruptor rather than how the company actually does it, and this is perhaps the great, largely untapped opportunity for you and your company.

So let's rewind for just a moment and set the scene.

The changing face of sales and marketing, and in fact the entire business world, has left many people and organizations floundering, unsure of how to achieve any degree of traction in a world where things haven't just 'changed' but instead the entire rulebook has been torn up and thrown away and 'disruption' has become the norm.

The old paradigms of how sales and marketing used to work simply don't hold true any more. Where once there were sales now there simply aren't, but on the other hand, new pockets of sales opportunities seem to be popping up all over the place. On the face of it, it seems to make no sense.

Certainly in the world of business, looking around at what is happening (or perhaps what has already happened), you could be forgiven for thinking that it makes no sense. Things seem to be changing everywhere and for agile young businesses this can present problems. However, for established businesses it presents a cliff face to climb. 'With so much to lose how can my company ever respond to these seismic shifts in how business, commerce (and indeed the entire world) operate?' But you must respond because standing still is simply not an option. The challenge is going to be to work out how you and your business can navigate through the minefield of change and how you can construct an argument that means that 'change' is on the agenda and has a sense of urgency.

The problems of today

For sales and marketing the unpredictability of what works, and what doesn't, means that for sales it's becoming extremely difficult to forecast accurately. For marketing it's becoming ever more difficult to create and run marketing campaigns in which you can have confidence in the outcome and surety of delivering a positive ROI.

Sales pipelines are often filled with hopes and dreams. Deals that are 'in the bag' fall away at the last moment and 'bluebirds' (sales that have come out of nowhere) are popping up to help save the salesperson's hide.

For marketing departments campaigns that have worked for years – running events, direct mail, advertising, telesales – simply can't get traction; like the salesperson's 'bluebird' deals sometimes these events can deliver a massive success… but more often than not they don't and sometimes they deliver nothing at all. The worry here, like in the sales department, is that there seems to be no rhyme nor reason to what happens; it's like spinning the roulette wheel.

The dynamics of the new, digitally enhanced world mean that 'best practice' is a thing of the past. We don't mean that there isn't excellence, but the processes that used to be considered 'the way to do it' seem at best rather outdated now and the fact that what you did yesterday doesn't work today has cast a veil of concern over much of what these functions can offer, even within the most established of businesses.

It's not about apps

In this sea of uncertainty, we see the arrival of clever apps and new products which change industries (or create new industries) overnight. Often we identify these as being the cutting edge of disruption and they certainly are part of the disruption process. But there are bigger things at play than just apps and products.

Yes, apps such as Uber and Airbnb are part of a trend that we're seeing, but the underlying cause of this trend is the change in consumer sophistication and consumer behaviour. Anyone who has used the Uber app will appreciate that the app itself is nice, but that's not the reason we gravitate towards using it rather than flagging down a passing taxi. The fact that we can see the rating for the driver, the fact we get the route we took (and a receipt) e-mailed to us, the fact that we no longer need to carry cash (or tip the driver), the fact we no longer wait for 20 minutes in the rain for a cab that 'is just around the corner' to finally arrive. The Uber service, how it's presented, how relevant it is to our modern behaviours and how nice the user interface is are all reasons that we love it.

Companies that engender this level of 'comfort' in their customers – Airbnb, Amazon, Skype, every social network, Gmail, Spotify – have recognized that in the modern world they are not selling a product; instead they are 'marketing and selling' a product. With Uber you get in a car for a lift, with Airbnb you stay in a room/apartment, with Amazon you buy a product... the companies are simply sales and marking engines and to be relevant today and in the future YOU need to be a sales and marketing engine for your company's product.

We can all see this is true because we know how our own behaviours have changed over the years. We know that we interact with the buying process very differently than how we did a decade or more ago. We ALL see this. But for some reason, whilst everyone within your organization acknowledges this, the organization itself probably finds this realization very difficult to embrace and adapt to.

Because the front-facing part of the interaction with the Ubers of this world is the app, many organizations see this as being the solution rather than just the interface. How many times have you sat in a meeting where someone says, 'what we need is an app'? I'll wager it's a lot. This is because the app is seen as the disruptor rather than the underlying process, product or ethos. Of course, an app to bring together a customer or prospect with an outdated and irrelevant organization (or rather what's perceived as an outdated and irrelevant organization) is unlikely to get much traction in the modern world, a world where people have a short attention span and expect to be the focus of the conversation, but nonetheless we keep building apps.

We see this often: organizations are typically focusing on the technology as if it were the solution (not just apps – marketing automation, new websites, ERP and BI systems...), which of course it is not. These tools or technologies are merely the enabler or the gateway and if they enable easier access to something that isn't attractive then they aren't adding any value.

There's no silver bullet

We often forget (or choose to forget) that there is no such thing as a silver bullet, a panacea that can cure all ills. We're not saying that technology isn't important as an enabler of this change, because it is.

Technology is a vital platform or launch pad for this success, but often organizations embrace technology as if it is of itself the solution. As if it is the technology that will catapult the organization from laggard to early adopter; as if it will compensate for many of the organizational shortcomings with which they are battling. But it won't. 'A fool with a tool is still a fool', as Grady Booch once said, and never is it more true than in hoping that the shiny new tech tool the business is planning to use will do anything other than speed the inevitable decline.

When we work with organizations the issue we often see is that they simply haven't moved with the times. The acknowledgement that their customers (and consumers in general) make their buying decisions in a profoundly different way to how they did in the past is accepted, but somehow this hasn't percolated down to be reflected in the organizational change which should have occurred for them to remain relevant to these customers.

It probably is not that the organization is in denial, but more that it simply doesn't know where to start in the process of re-engaging the audience that they once had but have now probably lost.

We see this rudderless behaviour more than ever in the customer-facing areas of sales and marketing and it is here that organizations arguably should begin their transformation. Here is where they likely will get the biggest payback for their efforts in the shortest timeframe because it is where they are most likely to be seen by their customers, and is the engine for generating revenue to prove that the transformation is working.

There has always been some tension between sales and marketing (which you could argue has driven higher performance in the past) but that tension has made them inefficient and unsuited to customer needs in 2018 and beyond. They are somewhat entrenched in the old ways of doing things. Perhaps they feel that things will change back to how they were? Perhaps they feel that this is just a glitch and that 'normal service will be resumed shortly'? But certainly they usually seem to be unable to make the fundamental changes they need to in order to reinvigorate what they do. They are often simply going through the motions (or perhaps they are deluded). They know it's not working but they keep doing it nonetheless.

Patient: Doctor, doctor, my wife thinks she's a chicken.
Doctor: Sir, you should have her committed.
Patient: We would… but we need the eggs.

Anyone who has read about the history of marketing knows that huge businesses were built on great marketing; it used to be the engine that powered success – have a look at the TV Industrial Complex hypothesis suggested by Seth Godin in his TED talk. But that was then and this is now. That great powerhouse of business growth and market share has in many instances become a shadow of its former self. It has been reduced to a department focused on producing brochures (which nobody reads/believes) or organizing events (which nobody attends).

But the 'fault' for the business woes created by the failure of this part of the engine is not solely with marketing (although some of it is).

Sales is also to blame. We have salespeople who make their unsuspecting customers (or victims) buy products that they don't need in order that the seller can make their numbers and retain their job. The salesperson has lost the position of 'confidant and friend' or 'trusted advisor' and has become, in many cases, someone to be avoided rather than embraced.

Is this cynical?

Yes, this is quite a cynical view of how marketing and sales departments operate in the modern world, but there's certainly some evidence to suggest this is in fact the root cause of many of the issues.

For some years these departments have viewed each other with suspicion and distain rather than as part of an integrated customer-centric function designed to support the revenue engine of the business and delight the buyer. Where once there was an expectation of marketing and sales in the customers' eyes, now the marketing material is to be avoided at all costs and the salesperson too. Now marketing is an endless stream of platitudes designed to tick boxes rather than add value to the reader/viewer, and the sales teams have got a bad name for themselves.

Businesses largely have, over time, taken the easy option. They have not made the changes that they know they have needed to make in the sales and marketing departments because perhaps it hasn't fitted with the 'corporate structure' or because making the changes should be done after I have left the company as I have only a few more years before retirement and those things are 'still kinda working'. Certainly, whatever the reason, businesses have updated and modernized much of what they do: real-time business intelligence, enterprise resource planning, human resources systems, distribution and supply chain and much more, but not sales and marketing for some reason.

The sales and marketing functions of businesses are doing pretty much the same thing that they have been doing for 50 years and as a result of this they simply don't add the value that they once did.

So, if sales and marketing are irrelevant in their current form what should they do?

Clearly people still need to sell... and the marketing function still has a purpose? Yes, of course. Sales is the most valuable department within any organization because cash is the lifeblood of every business. Marketing needs to find a way to support that function in a more efficient, more focused and less political manner.

What businesses need is the merging of sales and marking departments to create a new department (or perhaps a new operational model) where sales and marketing work hand in hand to deliver sales, value and visibility in a truly customer-focused way. The marketing department needs to provide the sales teams with the material they need in the real world in a timely and suitable manner and the sales department needs to tell the marketing team what they need, and not just on the day they need it, so that marketing can produce material which actually works.

If the marketing support that sales have asked for doesn't yield a sale, then there needs to be an open and frank dialogue about what went wrong and how it can be better the next time. There needs to be an attitude of team spirit and not an attitude of 'them and us'.

The business case for Smarketing

This book provides you with a methodology, process and the tools to make your organization a Smarketing-based one. The buying process has changed, driven by the internet and the ability of the buyer to gain instant information. But it has also been driven by Millennials and Generation Z, who, just like their parents before them, have different expectations of the world. Tim's mother, who is 80 years old, recalls the shock of Bill Haley and The Comets and Elvis Presley. Every generation changes, whether it's the Sex Pistols, Britney Spears, The Spice Girls or One Direction.

Why would you change to become a Smarketing organization?

With the dysfunction now in the buying process, the worse case for not embracing Smarketing is that you will go out of business; if you are not going out of business then maybe you could become irrelevant. Of course, the fact you are reading this book means it's highly likely that you will implement the methodology or will try hard to.

We live in a hyper-competitive world where companies compete on the basis that they have a better product and better service than anyone else, but in fact the buyer sees that all products and services are equal. There is no difference. For a company to still be in business today, they have to provide value, and it is this value that differentiates and provides profit for the seller organization.

Seller competitive advantage

To really be different from your competitors and have a competitive advantage requires you to market and sell differently. Buyers want to be educated, they want insight, and they want to know industry trends and how you can make an impact. Not at a product or feature/function way, but as business leader to business leader. This requires sales and marketing to work together in terms of co-creating content, in the hand-off of leads, and in building business relationships, as well as building trust and collaboration within customers and accounts.

Connecting the customer journey

The modern buyer interacts with businesses in many different ways. We can be researching a product or service on the train on the way to work; reading content, surfing websites all on our mobile. We then go into work and can be doing the same on our work PC, then more research on the mobile on the way home, making the purchase when we get home by calling up the company.

As marketers and sellers we have to look at our customers holistically, understanding that people want to buy over different channels, but also want to consume different content: long-form, short-form, video, etc. The need now is greater than ever to make sure we 'connect the dots' to make sure we have the right resource, marketing, pre-sales, expert, salesperson in the right place at the right time to help the buyer to buy. No longer can we decide who interacts with the buyer as we are not deciding where the buyer is. The competition is, after all, just one click away. How many times have you tried to purchase something but have gone to the competition because a company makes it too hard for you to buy?

The business case

For any reader of this book, at some point somebody is going to ask you, 'Why Smarketing?'; you can give those examples above, and they are all good reasons, but really, people will want to know, why financially?

So without building a business case, which is probably different for each organization, here are some financial reasons to go Smarketing.

Win–loss ratio – win more than you lose

Connecting with clients right through the funnel, having no hand-off and getting the right resource to the client at the right time will create a major competitive advantage. Your organization will naturally be seen as the solution to a client's problem, earlier in the buying cycle. You should in fact be able to stand out and get business before the competition are involved and therefore at a higher margin.

Share of wallet

In Chapter 10 we talk about share of wallet (SoW) in more detail, the impact being that once you have a client, Smarketing will enable you to get more repeat business and referrals. In addition, existing clients should come back to you to buy over and over again. The Account-Based Marketing (ABM) methodology we talk about in Chapter 10 will explain more.

Resources and efficiency

We also cover this later in the book but there is no marketing or sales department out there that has too many resources. We outline how moving to Smarketing is a more efficient way to work and to maximize the use of both human and capital resources in the business. This is a very important factor in justifying this transformation and should be near the top of the list when looking at why to change.

Employee development and attracting the best talent

Smarketing and implementing some of the provisions with human resources (HR) discussed in Chapter 11 should enable you to switch your current recruitment from push to pull. Many companies think that recruitment is about posting jobs on social media: this is a push model. If we create an environment where through the use of social media and employee advocacy people are actually queuing up to work for you, then you will be the employer of choice in your industry.

Research and development (R&D)

By activating advocates of yours through social media, you are able to get them to talk about how great you are, which other social media users will pick up – great for your brand and sales. In addition, you can also get their feedback on yours and your competitors' products. This input into R&D should mean you have the best market-led products in the market.

In summary, the business case should mean you have the most margin, the most loyal customers, the best talent and the best products. We realize this all sounds too good to be true; please buckle up and read on as we think there is something truly remarkable about Smarketing and we hope when you have read this you will too.

Move fast and break things

Facebook launched with this famous motto, which refers to Mark Zuckerberg's love of the 'fail fast' system. Try something, and if it doesn't work, throw it away and try again. You could consider this in a slightly different light in 2018 though. Now businesses fail FAST. Businesses move from working to not working if they aren't agile enough to be able to respond to changes in the market and changes in their customers' behaviour. A competitive advantage is good, status quo is bad, competitive disadvantage is corporate suicide. Businesses have to be looking for ways to improve engagement and efficiency and we believe that Smarketing is an obvious way to do both.

Introducing 'Smarketing', the future that every business needs to understand

If you have got this far, then thank you; please can we ask you a big favour? Share with us a selfie of you and the book tagging in @timothy_hughes, @agsocialmedia and @HugoW_Oracle, or just a photo of the book, but please tag us in and say 'Hi!'.

Questions to ask yourself

1 Is your organization involved in a digital transformation? If so, is the leadership involved and leading from the front? If not, what could you, as a change agent, do to change this?

2 Does your company have a mindset for change? If not, what activities could you instigate that will help change the mindset?

3 Which stakeholders will you need to talk to about this change and what are the different ways in which you need to talk to them? A finance director will be motivated differently to, say, a marketing director.

4 What will be the best way to evoke this change in your business – face to face, through webinar or both? It may be that your business is based all on one site, or is global, with many different sites.

5 What cultural sensitivities will you need to take into account if you are discussing change?

Reference

Capgemini Consulting (2015) When digital disruption strikes: How can incumbents respond? (Published on Twitter 10 May 2015 – 6:25 pm) [Last accessed 16 May 2018]

Why marketing in its current form is dead 01

As co-authors of this book we have both salespeople and marketers represented so there is always that different view of the world vying for the upper hand. Marketers tend to be quite analytical people – anecdotal evidence is fine but 'show me the data', the hard facts – whereas salespeople tend to be more hands-on and 'learn on the job' kind of folk.

Marketers interrogate things, not just at a micro level such as individual campaigns, but at a macro level such as strategies and the entire marketing world. And it is this analytical bent that often leads them to the inexorable conclusion that marketing, in its current form, is dead. Not in its death throes, but already dead; it is just that many marketing departments have not yet realized it. Like the chicken running around the farmyard with its head cut off, marketing is simply going through the motions. Like the ceremonial guards at the royal palace, marketing has become a rather outmoded and irrelevant exercise.

Let's tell a story

To explain this rather controversial standpoint let's tell a story.

In the very earliest days of 'modern' marketing (which was largely advertising in those early days) advertising geniuses like J Walter Thompson, then Leo Burnett, then Raymond Rubicam and David Ogilvy pioneered and refined through testing and research the concept and the delivery of messages in a way that was startlingly simple and effective. This was 'interruption marketing'. It works like this. I, the marketer/advertiser, craft a message and then buy media space to place that message in front of you, my target audience. I spend the profits from the sales this generates on buying more media space. I then spend the profits that *that* generates on buying more media space and so on.

Seth Godin, the US marketing guru, famously coined this process 'the TV industrial complex' in his famous TED talk of February 2003.

> I call it the 'TV-industrial complex'. The way the TV industrial complex works, is you buy some ads, interrupt some people, that gets you distribution. You use the distribution you get to sell more products. You take the profit from that to buy more ads. And it goes around and around and around, the same way that the military-industrial complex worked a long time ago. (Godin, 2003)

It is this spiral of media buying which created household brands such as Kellogg's, Persil and Coca-Cola. The success of this technique was well proven from the early 20th century through to the 1970s and even the 1980s.

This basic concept of 'interruption marketing' has been the foundation for most marketing. I 'interrupt' you with my message and there's a chance that you will respond to that and if I do it often enough I can effect a behavioural change in you and make you buy my product or service.

As time passed, and new platforms and technologies emerged, marketers realized that there were other ways of delivering the message. There was above the line (advertising – TV, radio, outdoor, print ads) and now there was below the line (everything else – PR, SEO, paid search, events, content marketing, etc).

Despite this new marketing world, however, still the same basic rules held true. You crafted a message and that message was delivered (and believed) and customers bought. For a long time nothing much changed in the world of marketing. Yes, marketers got smarter and used more sophisticated techniques – segmentation, different types of campaigns, celebrity endorsements, sponsorship – but basically there was still a very strong correlation between eyeballs and sales. As more competitors appeared those eyeballs were divided amongst

Figure 1.1   Marketing interrupts everything © Digital Leadership Associates

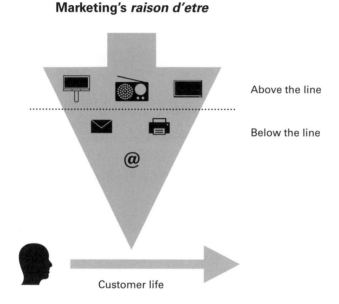

Marketing's *raison d'etre*

Above the line

Below the line

Customer life

the competition but this was easily overcome by either advertising/ marketing in new places or by simply buying more eyeballs (paying for more ads, more mail shots, etc).

Because these same basic cornerstones of the marketing world went unchallenged for so long, there was never a need to fundamentally change what marketers did.

Bigger and better = more sales

Better creative campaigns = more sales. Bigger ad spend = more sales. More names on the mailing list = more sales and so on.

The advent of digital communication has given marketers the chance to be significantly more sophisticated in what they do and how they do it. The immediacy of digital (and the two-way nature of digital channels) has meant that marketing departments have been able to measure more accurately what's working and amend things in real time; this has driven increased efficiency and increased ROI (within certain parameters).

Marketers have also been quick to pounce on the other benefits of digital marketing, such as an evaporation of their delivery costs for below-the-line campaigns and a huge reduction in above-the-line too. But despite this revolution provided by the digital channels, still the same fundamental dynamics of the marketing world have remained unchallenged.

Because of this, organizations generally have centralized 'corporate' marketing departments. The purpose of these departments has been to ensure uniformity of message (to support the larger brand vision/company objectives) and to 'police' the quality and appropriateness of the corporate communications. This makes perfect sense from the corporate perspective.

These marketing departments produce centralized brochures and information, centralized advertising and a centralized message. They may also produce departmental or industry vertical campaigns and literature too. But it is still all run and designed to provide uniformity. Economies of scale in terms of both costs and, perhaps more importantly, thinking.

For a long time this was perfectly sufficient; in fact for a long time this was brilliant. This type of marketing was able to drive the growth and sales of the world's largest companies – Procter & Gamble, Johnson & Johnson, GE, BP, Ford, etc, but 10 or so years ago things began to change. If you work in marketing you will have seen this; over the last decade a seismic shift has occurred in both how successful campaigns are and how unpredictable this success is.

Whilst the advent of digital has seen a fundamental change in how marketers have operated, the most fundamental change facing marketing departments has not been the technology but has been within the very customers with whom they have been trying to have a conversation. Those customers simply do not trust or believe what the marketer says any more.

The trust has gone

Studies show that over 75 per cent of people don't believe advertising any more.

Forbes reported research by LAB42 (2013) as:

- 96 per cent of respondents think half or more weight-loss ads are photoshopped;
- 76 per cent of said ads in general were either 'very exaggerated' or 'somewhat exaggerated';
- 87 per cent think half or more cleaning ads are photoshopped.

Think about it, that means that more than 7 out of 10 people who hear the marketer's message don't think that they're being told the truth. If you are really honest, you know this to be true: 'the best lager in the world', 'the ultimate driving machine', really? You don't believe it and neither do other customers. This doesn't take anything away from the creative brilliance of the strapline or the campaign as a whole but it does mean that the people being marketed to simply don't lap it up in the way that they did a few years ago.

In the Nielsen Trust in Advertising report 2015 (Nielsen, 2015) extensive research shows that with the exception of personal recommendation, pretty much all forms of media are trusted about 50 per cent of the time.

As reported by Digiday, Rakuten Marketing research from July 2017 showed that ads are lumped in the same bucket as fake news – online advertising was regarded as a disruptive experience by 83 per cent of the 2,500 people polled and, perhaps more tellingly, 63 per cent of people positively 'distrust advertising' (Davies, 2017).

Rhiannon Prothero – Marketing Director UK & Ireland, SAP

… because of this we have to have a different conversation, we have to pull ourselves into an environment for discussion. By us I mean marketing and sales, into an environment for discussion with the customer that no one else can have. This is a conversation that only we can have. We drive the world of SAP capabilities down into something relevant for this specific group of customers and for simplicity we've gone for industry (because we have to group them somehow) and that's where we say we think we've uncovered something not only highly compelling but unique. Then we take that to sales and say if you want to create an opportunity in your customer, or close an opportunity, this is the message you need to be giving, these are the conversations you need to be having.

Before we explore why the trust has broken down, we should consider the pressures that consumers are now under that simply weren't there before. Pressures that are adversely affecting their ability to interact with your marketing, your messages and your brand.

Everyone is time poor

When I was growing up (not that long ago) the world was a very different place. There was a slower pace of life. People weren't living in a hyperconnected world. People were 'out of contact' for large portions of their days and to be frank everything just seemed a little bit more leisurely.

Now there is a huge weight of expectation on everyone's shoulders: work, career, family, hobbies, health & fitness. There's television, console games, portable games, music everywhere. Nobody in the modern world ever says 'I have an afternoon free' because they don't any longer.

We don't have time to do the things we even consider leisure any more.

In just a five-year time span from 2011 to 2016, 18–24-year-olds watched TV one-and-a-half hours less each day, averaging at more than 10 hours weekly and 20 minutes daily (Nielsen, 2017).

By 2020, it is estimated that 18–24-year-olds will be watching just under two hours of TV a day (Deloitte Global, 2016).

Whilst this has huge ramifications for marketers (which we will look at in a moment) it also does for society and for humanity. In the same way that marketing budgets have been spread over more channels, so has people's time.

Everyone is time poor. This is a much overused phrase but it's overused for a reason. A few years ago you would 'wait' for your content: buying music, watching a film, seeing the news, receiving a response to your letter, getting that brochure in the post. Now you don't. Now everything is available to you *now*, from any supplier anywhere in the world. Now you have the entirety of humankind's knowledge at your fingertips 24/7, an infinity of things you can do with that spare minute. You can view every piece of video that has ever been shot or listen to every piece of music that has ever been recorded. You can watch every film or read every book and you can do it all now. Immediately. This very second.

So, against this backdrop, why would you want to waste some of your precious time reading *my* marketing material? Marketing material that talks about me rather than about you.

Seth Godin famously said, 'I have better things to do with my time than solve your marketing problems', and this is how we all feel to a greater or lesser extent. No longer are we prepared to wade through pages of turgid corporate speak in order to uncover the product features we are trying to find. Instead, we begin to read the company communications and if we're not immediately engaged or entertained or educated, we simply throw it in the bin and go elsewhere.

This is a very tough reality of communications in the modern world, and one which most marketing departments seem not to have grasped yet.

But it isn't just time that is the barrier.

Ignorance (information/knowledge scarcity)

For many years, marketing departments have had the knowledge. Their customers have been largely ignorant of what their products do, whether they are well regarded, reliable and well supported, and whether the competitors are better or worse. In fact, for many years the buyer had trouble even finding out who the main players in an industry or sector were.

Not anymore. Buyers are now knowledgeable. Buyers sometimes know more about the product or service than the seller. Certainly they are equipped with more information than they ever have been and this very clearly has changed the landscape in which sales and marketing operate. No longer is the role of the marketing department to weave mellifluous prose extoling the virtues of their products. Now, it would seem, the buyer has facts and comparisons, they have the hard data and they have it at their fingertips. So what do they want? Above all else what they want is help.

Now they want the seller to empathize with them and understand their issues and drivers; they want the seller to solve their problems and to create solutions. They don't want the seller to talk 'platitudes' or to talk about themselves; they want the seller to befriend them and genuinely help them. They want advice, impartiality (wherever possible), honesty and they want to be empowered to the point that they can be sure in their own minds that they are making the right decision.

You know that this is true. Whilst you may fight against it, you know this is how *you* behave. You don't believe company literature, or wade through loads of marketing speak even if you yourself are a marketer. What you want is someone you can trust to give you their 'expert' help and guidance.

Rhiannon Prothero – Marketing Director UK & Ireland, SAP

Do customers need to hear more about our great analytics? No. Do they need to hear about great opportunities to change their business in a way that will give them more customers? Yeah, I'd say they do.

That's my function in this mix, to make a judgement on how we continue to promote the notion that this is what we at SAP do. Elevating the conversation and making sure that the focus of that conversation is always the customer. That's my point about the constant juggle of who does what well in this big soup of what needs to happen, who is best placed in any given situation to get the best result; and that's why it's no good just 'saying' marketing and sales work really well together. You've got to be able to move in an agile fashion on basically every outcome, so you really have to work well together.

So how have things moved so far so quickly? Well, we suspect that you know the answer to that too. The internet. The internet allows your customers to go online and research. Not only can they go online and search for 'EPM software' or whatever it is they're looking for and find a list of marketing-led suggestions, through your efforts at pay-per-click advertising or banner ads, or search engine optimization, in short the things that you want them to find; they can also get to the 'soft underbelly' of your industry!

They can go online and they can see not just what you say about yourself (and what your competitors say about themselves) but also what other people say about you. They can see what, on the face of it, the 'impartial experts' say about your products and services. They can see what you want them to see, the great USP features, the things you're proud of, the case studies and success stories, but they can also see the stuff that you don't talk about. They can see the problem clients, the reliability problems, they can see the occasions when the whole support system you have worked hard to create has completely failed. They can see the things about which you are most ashamed. The internet has become the truth serum of purchasing decisions.

And, from the marketer's perspective, the worst part is that they can see all of this without you even knowing that they are looking. They can conduct their background research, they can self-educate, they can see what works in the real world, their world, they can compile a shortlist and a list of requirements and they can do all this without raising their head above the parapet. CEB (part now of Gartner research) has identified that in the B2B space the buyer is typically 57 per cent of the way through the buying journey before the seller even knows that they exist (this figure is quoted throughout the CEB website and is a crucial illustration of how the journey has changed) (CEB, 2018). Just think about that for a moment. Fifty-seven per cent. That means that in many cases your product may have been deselected and the purchase concluded without you ever even knowing that it was a missed opportunity.

Now the marketers may well argue that the buyer self-educated with *their* marketing material, but the truth is that they probably didn't. They went online and they found third-party content which was impartial. This content was not 'on brand' or 'highlighting USPs' in the way that in-house content might. It was simply honest, or perhaps perceived by the buyer as being honest, which, let's be realistic, is all that matters in the marketing world. In this instance it wasn't the truth that was important, it was what the buyer *thought* the truth was that was important!

Clearly this instance is the exception rather than the rule. Well, we like to think it is, but of course for every one of these instances of a 'bluebird' sale, or a lucky break, our competitors may get 10, or 100, or 1,000, but let's assume for the moment that this doesn't happen very often.

The important lesson here is that the very concept of the customer journey probably isn't where we would like to think it is. The idea that *we* drive this, that we feed in the information when the customer needs to see it, that we are in control, is a complete fallacy. Today, the customer is in control and the marketing department could arguably be reduced to sending out brochures when, or perhaps IF, the customer requests them and very little more.

The biggest concern for marketing departments, though, is that with customers going online and self-educating, with them not announcing an intent to buy and effectively marketing and selling to themselves, is there any point in the future for marketing departments?

People don't believe advertising – not just going by the statistics we saw earlier that show that more than 75 per cent of people polled say they don't, but by the fact that the advertising industry simply cannot sell ad space the way that it used to.

A few years ago we saw the first real evidence of this when there was a 'TV advert advertising TV adverts'. This isn't a typo. The advert was telling us how valuable TV advertising was to brands. Clearly the most likely explanation for this was that they had advertising space that they couldn't sell, so they decided to make use of it by advertising themselves.

Fewer TV ad campaigns are generating a positive ROI. In a survey of 1,015 adults by ORC International, in conjunction with ad-tech firm Mirriad, 76 per cent reported blocking ads online and skipping traditional TV ads (Orc International, nd).

This is supported by many other pieces of research. In the October 2016 US News & World Report detailing MTV's current management problems, Associated Press shared the (then) latest Nielsen figures from what had once been the most popular teen network. At the end of September 2016, MTV averaged 550,000 prime-time viewers, down from its 2011 heyday figures of 1.48 million. For its most important demographic (18–34-year-olds; millennials), viewership declined nearly 25 per cent just in the year 2017.

But the interesting thing is that despite this sort of information being widely available and a pretty much universal acknowledgement that the whole advertising industry is in decline, marketing departments still see advertising (and TV advertising in particular) as being the most glamorous weapon in their arsenal and the poster child for what they do.

Headlines like 'WPP faces worst year in a decade as advertisers cut spending' (Sweney, 2017) and the fact that they (WPP) have issued profit warnings for three out of the last four quarters help underline the scale of the problem.

The fact is that industry experts see this problem increasing rather than reducing. 'We are facing something really different today. The pace of decline is accelerating because of new sources,' said Tom Rogers, the executive chairman of WinView Games and chairman and CEO of TRget Media, when we spoke at the 2017 Beet TV leadership summit on video advertising. 'Because of Netflix, Amazon, etc, year-over-year there is a vast decline in traditional television viewing and it will accelerate.'

You could argue that this 'blindness to the facts' underlines the fact that marketing departments really are eating their own dog food – they believe that perception is more important than truth because if they didn't, they would be acting differently. Possibly the advertising part of marketing is a perfect illustration of style over substance.

Surely, then, the thing that marketing departments should be more focused on is not advertising, but below-the-line campaigns, which have always been more targeted and 'intimate', right? They will be able to take up the slack from the gradual, or not so gradual, erosion of advertising effectiveness, yes?

Wrong again!

The bad news for marketing departments is that this reduction in effectiveness is not just limited to the intrusion in our lives that is advertising.

Fournaise Group research shows that in the first half of 2011, consumer response rates to not just advertising, but marketing communications as a whole, fell by an average of 19 per cent in countries including the United States, Europe and Australia (when measured against the first half of 2010), and also declined by 16 per cent in developing markets like India and China. So this failing of advertising is now being followed by a failure in other marketing too (Fournaise Marketing Group, 2011).

The truth is that people simply don't want to be hammered by communications all the time. Once again, think about your own situation.

You have a 'spam filter' on your e-mail inbox, which makes it more difficult for me to send you my electronic direct mail; more often than not the default setting for e-mails arriving from sources that aren't in your address book is that they go straight into the spam folder. For other e-mails, increasingly mail clients such as Apple Mail, or Outlook, have an 'unsubscribe' link added to all incoming generic mails which don't have one coded into the footer.

At home, you keep the recycling bin next to the front door so that all of the postal 'junk mail' can be put straight in there without you having to walk it all the way to the bin in the kitchen.

On your landline and mobile you have voicemail so you can screen incoming calls and call back people you want to speak to and ignore people you don't. And anyone who has ever tried cold-calling or telemarketing will know that the challenge is not finding people to phone, it is finding people who pick up the phone when you call them.

The fact that you use a DVR (digital video recorder) means that you don't need to even watch TV ads if you prerecord your viewing (or even make a cup of tea once your programme starts so you can buffer it). Although in fairness to this, social media and the concept of second (or third) screens is perhaps driving people back to watching things as they are being broadcast (but more of that later).

With the use of AdBlockers, even banner ads can be excluded from your life. Once again, Apple is leading the way in this technology by ensuring that when using Safari, cookies that allow tracking from website to website cannot be placed (so the days of that spotty teapot or embarrassing pairs of trousers you once viewed following you around the internet forever have passed!).

There's another Kogan Page book – *Native Advertising* by Dale Lovell – that covers this in depth.

Against this background, what chance does marketing in its current form stand? It seems that technology and behaviours are conspiring against marketing departments to make life very difficult.

And just when you think things cannot get any worse, along comes increased legislation. In the UK and Europe we have GDPR (General Data Protection Regulations) and there are similar initiatives being enacted across the globe. GDPR places exceptionally strict rules on the data you as an organization can store about your customers and prospects. Now, a breach of the security around this data carries strict penalties – both financial and criminal – for the directors and the company. So the databases you have spent years building, of your loyal customers, those for whom you have already been able to break down the barriers against marketing, may well become unusable.

If you don't believe us, some of the more innovative companies have seen this and have thrown away the playbook that their marketing departments have been using for decades.

Last week 23 June, JD Wetherspoon announced that it will stop sending newsletters via e-mail and has deleted its entire email mailing list. Chief Executive John Hutson announced it in an email to subscribers:

'Many companies use e-mail to promote themselves, but we don't want to take this approach – which they may consider intrusive.'

He added, 'Our database of customers' email addresses, including yours, will be deleted.'

The firm suffered a data breach of their customer database in 2015, where a third party stole personal data of 656,723 customers. The data contained personal data potentially compromising customers' names, e-mail addresses, dates of birth and phone numbers.

Reported in GDPR news (Edwards, 2017).

JD Wetherspoon is the largest pub/bar chain in the UK and it's interesting to see that they found themselves in a position where the risk/reward ratio has moved away from a large database being a benefit to it being seen as a liability. In that final e-mail they sent out they stated that customer details were being removed permanently and that customers who want to stay in touch should visit the website.

A brave move? Or just a sign of the times? We'll let you be the judge of that but it does suggest that perhaps the time-honoured marketing cornerstones are crumbling, or have perhaps already crumbled.

Either way, clearly the times are changing (or have changed) and the whole idea of the role of a marketing department is being rewritten on an almost daily basis.

The problem, you could argue, is that the marketing department as we know it hasn't adapted with the times. Yes, they have clearly embraced new technology, but in fact perhaps almost too readily, and therein may lie part of the problem.

Marketing departments have started to use automation tools, PPC micro-niching techniques, the Google partner network, personalized content, split testing and predictive analytics. They have then sought out co-branding opportunities to spend their 'influence' and have used data management platforms to find whole new worlds of audiences. Marketing departments have jumped at so many of these new technologies and folded them into their processes, workflows and structures, but, and this is a big 'but', they have seldom stopped to consider what the customer wants. They have seldom stopped to think whether this behaviour has enriched the customer experience, and they've failed to 'ruthlessly put themselves in their customers' shoes'; instead they have simply ploughed on regardless. They have very much embraced the belief that the end justifies the means and have so often dived on the latest technological improvement, not for the betterment of the customers' experience but to either make their own lives easier or to make their sales numbers.

That may seem like an incredibly negative view of marketing, but some of us are marketers and have a huge fondness for it; however, we believe that the comments we've made are rooted very firmly in fact.

You certainly shouldn't feel sorry for marketing departments though, because they have been the architects of their own demise and because there is a brave new world coming (in future chapters) where you will see a different way of viewing the marketing function which absolutely delivers on the customer-first vision that marketing should always have been. But for now that simply isn't happening and marketing continues in its old form, gradually dying a slow and painful death.

Figure 1.2   Reducing distribution costs © Digital Leadership Associates

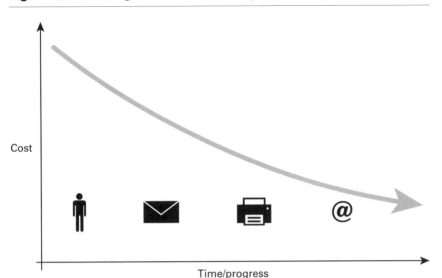

Think about what Seth Godin famously once said in his TED talk: 'The problem with marketers is that they break everything'; that is, for the most part, the truth. What Seth is saying isn't that marketers don't deliberately destroy things, but more that they often milk them dry. Look back over the development of marketing as new channels have become available.

It used to be events and sampling but in time it became direct mail in one form or another. After the era of printed direct mail, fax machines became tools to deliver the same mediocre message to more people at a lower cost. At the time it was a revelation. I could fax to my target market at a fraction of the cost of using traditional mail (because there were no longer print costs involved) and perhaps equally importantly, I could get a faster affirmation of whether the campaign was a success or not. Rather than having to wait two weeks to know if my idea was successful, with the adoption of the fax-blast I would know in just a few days.

After fax, e-mail became the channel to deliver the same mediocre message at a lower cost still. With e-mail marketing not only was there no cost whatsoever for sending out my message (with no telephone line cost like there was with the fax machine) but I could get that same affirmation of success, or failure, even faster… instead of it being just a few days, I would know in just a few hours whether my campaign was a success or not.

At each stage of 'progress' these new technologies have been hungrily consumed by marketers as a way of solving their immediate problems but seldom with much consideration for the long-term ramification of their actions.

Spam filters were created in response to organizations sending out an ever-increasing number of unsolicited e-mails. Regulations such as GDPR and the Telephone Preference Service were created as a response to individuals' data being sold for profit to other organizations. Ad blockers were created in response to advertisers conducting 'visual spamming' of their prospects. TiVO was created…

You see what I mean? Every action has an equal and opposite reaction. Nobody has ever said 'we need a pay rise filter' because staff are annoyed that every year they receive a pay rise! There is no great groundswell of desire for a 'discount blocker' or a 'Christmas gift filter' because these are things that everybody *does* want. These are things that add value. These are things that people smile about.

Not so with marketing because marketers are not doing something that people actually want; they are still frantically trying to interrupt people with their message in the same way that they did in the early days of advertising and marketing.

The great Gary Vaynerchuck talks about how he has banned everyone in his family from buying another Samsung product again 'until I am dead' because of their campaign which kept interrupting his viewing of the New York Jets' trade of a player which he was hoping to see on ESPN.com. It's worth a watch (GaryVee fans, 2017 – excuse the swearing) if you haven't seen it because it's funny and it gives an interesting narrative on how others view our marketing. The key takeaway is that because he kept clicking the ads (by mistake) the marketers were thinking 'wow look at this guy, he's really engaged and loves our product', where in fact, poor Gary was getting more and more annoyed that his big fingers meant he couldn't click the 'close ad' cross to see what he wanted to actually see.

This may well be a salutary lesson for all marketing departments but one I doubt they will take on board. The reason I say that is that marketing departments are extremely entrenched in their behaviours and beliefs. All departments have these (as do all people) but somehow the marketing department is slightly different from most. And the reason behind this is really simple.

In the early days of marketing it was often viewed as a strange type of alchemy. A wondrous thing where the marketing department would create a campaign full of beautiful images and prose, tell a story and customers would, as if by magic, arrive and spend money. This 'art' rather than 'science' view has persisted ever since. The board (who are often business people or accountants) have given the marketing department a budget every year to go away and generate impressions, views, share of voice, brand recognition, traffic... whatever else the marketing department has been selling, and for the most part the board either hasn't understood the process or hasn't cared. Marketing has failed to bring the senior stakeholders into the tent and make them champions, but has preferred to operate with some mystique.

In the late 1980s a friend/client of mine was the global head of advertising at the world's largest clothing manufacturer, you know who they are. He had some incredible successes (I think he may have been responsible for the guy taking off his jeans in the launderette and washing them to the strains of Marvin Gaye) but whilst this campaign, and several others delivered a staggering ROI, some didn't. The next advertising campaign featuring the guy moving from back yard to back yard swimming in everyone's pool was an abject failure. It was also extremely costly to make. But my point is that he was the maverick. He created a new type of narrative but he didn't draw in the senior players within the company because he didn't want to have his creative ideas diluted.

To a certain extent that is what marketing departments are famous for; they get given a budget to generate sales and... well, to be frank, they don't generate sales. What they do is generate the things we mentioned earlier – impressions, traffic, etc. They absolutely don't connect the dots for the people who fund them and consequently they are very much at risk (as we are now seeing).

Marketing departments need to be able to show categorically that they create revenue, that they deliver a positive ROI, that they are a profit centre and not a cost centre. They need to show $$ and not impressions. They shouldn't talk about how their campaigns have 'captured people's imaginations' or that the 'elegant new navigation on the website streamlines the customer experience' or that 'the new angular look of the corporate logotype will engage the millennials better than the old one' or whatever these nebulous, subjective and vanity measures might be. Instead they need facts. They need to be able to prove their worth. They need to be able to show that $X million of revenue is a direct result of the efforts this quarter. But sadly this is unlikely to happen, partly because these two sides of the brain are probably incompatible and partly because the full scale of the risk of not changing hasn't been seen and therefore there isn't the desire yet.

A few years ago a client we know was a mid-sized law firm. We had been working with them developing a social media strategy but they didn't feel that they had the resources to be able to write the content, send the tweets and manage any conversations that resulted from this. So they took me to see their agency for lunch. We sat down in a nice restaurant and the conversation went as follows:

Us: so what are you going to do for the client?

Agency: well we specialize in the legal sector so we will write some content and distribute it through the various social channels and that will create some 'noise' and from that we will get some sales...

Us: That's nice, but how are you going to prove that you are generating this noise and sales?

Agency: We specialize in the legal sector so we will write good content, really good content and that will create the buzz we need.

Us: You've said that but how are you going to PROVE it?

Agency: Because the content will be really good...

Needless to say the meal didn't end well because we were stuck in a circular argument. The agency believed that because it was (what they considered) good content, that would be enough. We tried to explain that 'good' is no barometer for success and that even if it was creating some buzz, not being able to prove the value of this was going to be a major problem. But the agency were very entrenched in their view of the world.

Conclusion

So, many marketing departments have, in our opinion, made their own bed. For some time now, the cornerstones of the whole marketing industry have been unsteady or crumbling: advertising not working like it used to, people being too busy to go to events (and there being too many events), falling response rates because audiences are inundated with content that they can't be bothered or don't have the time to read, people not believing centralized marketing stories, etc, etc, etc.

The signs have been there for several years but marketing departments have had their heads firmly buried in the sand. They have known the writing is on the wall (if they are really honest) but they probably haven't seen what the alternative is. They haven't yet identified what this shift needs to be.

Whilst the general gist of this chapter may at first glance come across as 'marketing is valueless', we certainly don't mean that; what we do feel though is that 'marketing departments' have largely become an irrelevance, rather like a slightly eccentric old aunt! What they haven't done is moved with the times.

So, is marketing a waste of time? NO, certainly not. Marketing provides a vital bridge between the company and the customer. It educates, it sells the blue sky vision of what's possible. It differentiates between the players in the same space. It facilitates so much of what an organization needs to do, but not in its current format.

Whilst marketing is vital, centralized marketing departments are dead, whether they know it or not. The management of the corporate website, Facebook page and Twitter profile will always need to be handled centrally. As will the production of the annual report and accounts and the shareholder communications, but everything else?

There must be a better way. And there is. And we are going to tell you what we think it is!

Questions to ask yourself

1 Is your corporate marketing currently broadcast? If so, what do you think you could do to make it less about you?

2 Do you have a true marketing strategy or is it a set of tactics that move on year after year?

3 Be honest with yourself: is your current marketing working or are there maybe things you need to dial up or dial down?

4 Asking question 3 in a different way: based on the changes in the way the internet impacts on the way we buy, and how legislation impacts on the way we treat data, are there current tactics you are employing in marketing that have reached the end of their shelf life?

5 What are your measures? Friends, Likes, Eyeballs, Leads, Meetings and Revenue? It's not for us to say which is right or wrong, but if you are reading this book, now is the time to take stock and decide if any changes need to take place.

References

CEB (Gartner) (2018) The digital evolution in B2B marketing, *CEB (Gartner)*. Available at: www.cebglobal.com/marketing-communications/digital-evolution.html [Last accessed 16 May 2018]

Davies, J (2017) The global state of consumer trust in advertising in 5 charts, *Digiday*. Available at: https://digiday.com/marketing/global-state-consumer-trust-advertising-5-charts/ [Last accessed 16 May 2018]

Deloitte Global (2016) Trailing millennials are the pro-C, not the post-PC generation (TMT Predictions 2016), *Deloitte*. Available at: www2.deloitte.com/cy/en/pages/technology-media-and-telecommunications/articles/tmt-pred16-tech-millennials-pro-pc-not-post-pc.html [Last accessed 16 May 2018]

Edwards, L (2017) JD Wetherspoon purposely deletes entire mailing list, *GDPR: Report*. Available at: https://gdpr.report/news/2017/06/30/jd-wetherspoon-purposely-deletes-entire-mailing-list [Last accessed 16 May 2018]

Fournaise Marketing Group (2011) Customer response to advertising fell by 19% in the first half of 2011: 3 reasons why. Available at: https://www.fournaisegroup.com/advertising-response-fell/ [Last accessed 25 June 2018]

GaryVee Fans (2017) Why I will never buy a Samsung again (Gary Vaynerchuk) [Video]. Available at: https://www.youtube.com/watch?v=HWg2VuTaxg8&feature=youtu.be [Last accessed 16 May 2018]

Godin, S (2003) How to get your ideas spread, *Ted Talks*. Available at: www.ted.com/talks/seth_godin_on_sliced_bread/up-next [Last accessed 16 May 2018]

Lab42 (2013) Does it really add up? *Lab42 blog*. Available at: http://blog.lab42.com/does-it-really-ad-up/ [Last accessed 16 May 2018]

Lovell, D (2017) *Native Advertising: The essential guide*, Kogan Page, London

Nielsen (2015) Global trust in advertising: Winning strategies for an evolving media landscape, *Neilson*. Available at: www.nielsen.com/content/dam/nielsenglobal/apac/docs/reports/2015/nielsen-global-trust-in-advertising-report-september-2015.pdf [Last accessed 16 May 2018]

Nielsen (2017) Traditional TB* viewing trends among 18–24-year-olds, *Marketing Charts*. Available at: www.marketingcharts.com/featured-24817/attachment/nielsen-traditional-tv-viewing-trends-18-24-yo-q12011-q22017-dec2017 [Last accessed 16 May 2018]

Orc International (nd) Survey finds 90% of people skip pre-roll ads. Available at: https://buff.ly/2jm6HN5 [Last accessed 20 June 2018]

Sweney, M (2017) WPP faces worst year in a decade as advertisers cut spending, *Guardian*. Available at https://buff.ly/2FyX8Ty [Last accessed 20 June 2018]

Why sales in its current form is dead

If people like you, they'll listen to you, but if they trust you, they'll do business with you.

ZIG ZIGLAR

We are living in the attention economy. As sales and marketers we are all looking to get people's attention: 'Buy my product, buy my product, buy my product.' In the previous chapter we looked at how traditional push marketing, invented in the 1930s but still the primary method of working, is no longer fit for purpose in the internet-empowered world.

As business leaders we must provide the leadership in our organization to make sure that our companies are selling in the best way. What do I mean by best? While it needs to meet the requirements of your market, it must also meet the needs of your customers in the most efficient way. Now nobody likes being sold to and nobody likes being interrupted; this must mean traditional push sales methods don't meet our clients' needs?

In this chapter we will continue developing the argument that sales in its current format is dead.

What exactly is social media?

A few years ago I was on holiday in Myanmar (Burma) and met a couple who knew very little about social media. It was during an evening meal, following an amazing train trip. The train took us from

Maymyo to Hsipaw, over the amazing Nyaung Pain crossing built by the British in 1903 over the Goktiek Gorge.

It was at dinner in Hsipaw that the subject of my work online and in social media came up.

In Myanmar, that morning we had needed to get up early and we had time to have a tea at a local tea house (it even had Wi-Fi). We walked up and down the station. When the train arrived an additional two carriages needed to be shunted from a siding and connected to the main train in the station.

That 20 minutes while we waited gave me time to wander alongside the train in the station and engage through the windows with the people on the train. In Burmese, 'Minglabar' is the standard welcome, similar to 'how are you?', 'good morning', etc. It is not time dependent, so you can use it at any time of the day.

Figure 2.1   Looking down the track at Maymyo station

Figure 2.2   Engaging with people on the Maymyo–Hsipaw train in Burma

The Burmese, I have found, are very friendly and are also keen to engage with 'outsiders' after the country being closed for so many years.

Walking down the outside of the train saying 'Minglabar' to the local people through the windows created new and different engagement with complete strangers. One family enjoyed having their photos taken with me showing them the results on the camera LCD screen – something they hadn't seen before. Many had not even seen their own photo before.

I found one lady who spoke some English and we talked: 'where was she going?', 'why was she travelling?' and 'how come she had learnt how to speak English?' I asked her. Simple questions but engaging all the same.

Back to the conversation at the dining table.

'Why,' I was asked 'would you want to talk on social media to people who are complete strangers?'

Relaying the story of the morning and the train journey, I think there was a 'light bulb' moment for my two dinner companions. Social media allows you to have a conversation; this can be person to person or from brand to person. It also allows people to ask questions. This can be with people you don't know or with your network of friends, family and wider contacts. Either way it's a conversation, an exchange, maybe of knowledge; it can enrich our lives. Maybe the

Figure 2.3   The train

latest joke will make us smile. But it can be used for the positive. It can of course be used for the negative, but the great thing about social media is that you are in control. You don't have to be friends with people or follow what people say. It is the ultimate in democracy. My followers can unfollow me at any time.

So what about sales?

George Best played in the English First Division. He played football (soccer) for Manchester United and his place of birth, Northern Ireland; some people will say he was one of the best footballers, certainly of his time, if not one of the best footballers ever. There's a story about how George had rented a room in one of London's top hotels to take his date at the time, the then Miss World. It therefore could have been argued at the time (stick with me on this) that this was the most beautiful woman in the world.

We have to remember that top footballers are today classed as athletes. They sleep, as do Olympic athletes, in oxygen tents, have chefs that make sure they eat a proper diet, get a good night's sleep and all the other things best-in-class athletes do. Not George Best.

He was going to live the high life, so he was in one of the best hotels in the world, with one of the world's most beautiful woman and a waiter arrives with the champagne. The waiter arrived, looked at George, Miss World and the vintage champagne he was delivering and said with no sense of irony, 'George, where did it all go wrong?' This is a metaphor for sales today. Sales as a profession has long been something to be proud of.

Sales, the 'good old days'

I recall being trained on Miller Heiman and Holden, but there are also methodologies such as SPIN. This was in the days where the buyer and seller 'knew the rules'. The only way you as a buyer could get information on a product or service was by calling up a company and talking to a salesperson or representative.

In the pre-internet world that Leo Burnett, the inventor of modern marketing, lived in, the only way you could get the details of your products and services in front of people was to tell them about it. You did this by advertising or with trade shows, conferences, etc. Or of course you cold-called.

We talk about this in more detail in future chapters but the way sales and marketing worked was that you told people about your products or services and you would broadcast. In addition, you would interrupt people to tell them. In a way, this was accepted; how else as a consumer would I find out about such things? Then the internet was invented and everything changed.

The birth of the empowered buyer

Consumers and buyers realized they had control; the internet empowered them to do their own research. Now if you see an advert about a product or service you can research, find and compare competitor products and often buy a competitor brand. This is the dichotomy for brands, that the power rests so much with consumers that your marketing efforts may actually drive those consumers and their money into the hands and the pockets of your competitors.

Buyers don't want to be sold to – none of us do

I recall as a student visiting Lanzarote. Not having any money and really wanting to see the island, I agreed to sit through a timeshare pitch, so I could get a coupon for three days' free car hire. It really was a showcase in sales. Asking questions about my requirements, the salesperson matched my requirements to the benefits of the timeshare. He even told us that his manager had said that if he didn't make this sale he would have to shave his moustache off. I'm not sure if that was true or him trying to get the sympathy vote, but he didn't get a sale and I got my car hire.

If we want to buy something now, we can go online and research it for ourselves. The first thing many of us do to get any question answered is reach for Google or maybe social media. This has placed immense power in the buyer's hands. If we take the Lanzarote example above, I can go online and research the prices of the properties from all the companies. I can also read all the good and bad news articles about buying a timeshare, so by the time I need to contact a company online I'm armed with a lot of information that I can ask the salesperson about. Often salespeople hear that from us and say, yeah, yeah, yeah, and then we will get a story about why things are different for their buyers. They are not.

Our buyers are not on social

We hear this all the time; at some meetings in Winnipeg we were told by an accountancy firm that none of their clients were on social. We went onto LinkedIn and found the number of CFO (Chief Financial Officers) in Canada and then the number in Winnipeg and it was exactly the same ratio. In fact, the proportion of CFOs active in the Winnipeg area was higher than in Canada as a whole. We also showed the client how many of those CFOs had recently changed jobs, posted on LinkedIn and appeared in the press. All of which could be reasons to contact them perhaps? We also showed them their alumni network; being ex-employees of the firm, they would be highly likely to take a request for a meeting. At the time of writing, over 40 per cent of the world's population is on social media and while your buyers may not be telling you they are on social media, they are.

We sell products that are...

Usually this involves people who sell to either big companies or small companies but basically, whatever they sell, for some reason people deem their customers to be not on social. For example, the small business owner who (as they are not on social) might assume that all the other small business are not on social either. Or people selling $100 million outsourcing/cloud contracts. Why would you search on the internet for those? In fact, we see people searching all the time.

Buying products requires you to burn through internal political capital. If, for example, you are going to take a report to the board about the purchase of a $100 million outsourcing contract that will change the internal landscape of your business and will probably transfer people from your company to the new outsourcing company, I can guarantee this will require somebody to go onto the internet. Why? If you are going to present to the board or be on the project, any professional person will want to have researched every angle. Be able to answer any question that the board may ask, plus make sure the project comes in on time and on budget. Your career may depend on it.

Treat me like an individual

As buyers we want to be treated like individuals, but this is nothing new. In his 1999 book *Permission Marketing*, Seth Godin argues that brands need to treat people as individuals, that is connect with people on a one-to-one basis. As we write there is a marketing term, 'hyperconnected', being used; the means of treating me as an individual were available in 1999.

From a B2B (business to business) perspective, in 1999 the book *The One to One Field Book* by Don Peppers and Martha Rogers was also published, making the case for consumers to be treated like the smart people we are.

The revolution in B2B buying

Every year CEB, now Gartner, undertakes research of the B2B buying process across the world and looks at different buying habits and patterns.

In 2017, they found that most B2B buyers are now 57 per cent of the way through the buying process by the time they contact a salesperson. This is a fundamental change from the days when I started selling, where the only way you could find out about my products and services was to ring me up and talk to me.

The empowered buyer

This also offers companies (big and small) the opportunity (rather than advertise and go to trade shows) to let people find out about your products and services as they surf the internet. People might find your white paper on Google, find your employees talking on LinkedIn about what a great company you are, or your customers recommending you on Twitter. Or, as I found out recently when I spoke at a company's sales kick off, when somebody searched for a 'social selling speaker' on YouTube.

Sometimes when I have posted this on LinkedIn, people think this research is old. I can only assume that they think that maybe this internet thing is just a fad and has gone away. This figure has held true for a number of years. In fact, a search on Google will bring up many different figures that people will spend time online doing research; the overwhelming evidence is that we do and so do our customers.

We talked earlier about the B2B Enterprise Accountancy salesperson who was called up by somebody wanting to buy their product. No demo; they had read the content on the internet and wanted to buy.

There is an interesting Gartner report from 2016 worth reading, called '94% = Enterprise buying teams that have abandoned a buying effort with no decision (in the past 2 years)' (Barnes, 2016).

I remember sitting with the human resources (HR) software sales team in my last company and somebody came back to the office and said, 'I'm glad that meeting is over, they knew more than me'. I seemed to be the only person not surprised. Of course, any evaluation team will have read up before a supplier turned up. In another instance, we visited, let's call them a 'big 5' company, and they said the internet didn't matter to them. They had relationships with CEOs and business was conducted between them and the CEOs. This surprised us too. We are aware of another 'big 5' that had a pricing proposal rejected by a customer as the people and the day rates they proposed did not match their corresponding LinkedIn profiles. For example, some of the people on the team were on LinkedIn as graduates and the proposal had pitched them in at a higher rate. The client rejected the proposal.

The 37 per cent rule

The other issue for salespeople that often isn't explained is the 37 per cent figure (Spenner and Schmidt, 2015).

If we think about when we purchase online, our search starts with us knowing nothing or little about what we are buying, then we (consume) content. We read articles and watch YouTube videos or even configure the car online, and we start becoming more and more educated about what we want to buy, to the point that when we are 37 per cent of the way through the buying process we understand what we want. We understand our requirements. But does the online buying process ever stop? We would argue that customers are socially active for 100 per cent of the buying process. Put another way, this is where social marketing meets social selling.

A sales director friend of mine came to me and asked for my help; he added:

We have deals where we get inbound around product X and we take the sale through 70 per cent of the way through the buying process. In many cases we are the only supplier. Then 70 per cent of the way through the process, the competition appears from nowhere and we lose the deal.

We did an evaluation of the company's digital footprint. In this case the results were revealing. We presented our findings back to the sales leader.

'How important are products X, Y and Z to you?' I asked.
'We are seen as market leaders,' was his response.
'Interesting,' I responded.
'Go to Google and search on those phrases,' I said. So, he got out his laptop.

He searched and his company didn't appear. In fact, his company was on the sixth page of Google. The (smaller) competition was on page one. His response was two words, one of which was 'hell'. It was the same for all three products.

I continued: 'You clearly list the products on your website, but you have no digital presence.'

As we handed over the report we said, 'What's happening is that the sale goes through to the point of recommendation/business case. The customer is confirming your position by searching on Google and you don't appear. But your competition does. The only conclusion that the customer can jump to is that you don't play in that market. But your competition does.'

This is just one of many examples of how social (for sales and marketing) is important all the way through the buying process. It is also 'interesting' how in this case these leads are created by a BDR (business development representative). In other words, while cold-calling was working for this business, the effort is being killed by not being social.

Selling vs empowering

From my earliest memories of sales there was a macho side to it. Think of Alec Baldwin in the film *Glengarry Glen Ross*, where he explained that salespeople needed to be ABC, Always Be Closing. But does that work against the empowered buyer that has spent time researching online, or, as we often see, using the information online to de-select companies. The buyer isn't some gullible person that we can just convince we are 'in the area', pitch to and close. The buyer will have researched about your product, its competitors and will have probably seen pricing details as well as customer references, good and bad. They are pretty sure what they are getting into and you the seller are getting in their way. Seller beware.

This goes against everything we salespeople were taught; we try to sell at every stage. We cannot help it, and in fact it is a behaviour that to buyers is a massive turn-off.

The other piece of research that CEB, now Gartner mention in their 2016 report 'The Revolution in B2B Buying' (CEB Research, 2016), is that the buyer is totally confused. Two years ago the average number of people that were required in order to make a B2B decision was 5.4; the figure is now 6.8. The likelihood that that decision will be made? If there is one person involved then that decision has an 81 per cent chance of being made; if there are more than six people involved, the likelihood of it happening is 31 per cent. As a business owner, a sales leader and a salesperson, this places your current forecast at risk. The biggest competitor? Doing nothing or making no decision.

Why can nobody make decisions in the world of B2B buying?

The modern buyer is often totally confused. The number of applications that can be purchased has accelerated. If we look at the marketing technology (Martech) space, in 2011 the category didn't exist; now there are over 5,000 products that are vying for a customer's time, attention and budget. This is growing all the time (Google Docs, nd).

For example, in 2011 there were 150 products that called themselves Martech; in 2012 there were 350; in 2014, 1,000; in 2015, 2,000; and in 2017 there were 5,000.

If you look at a sub-category of, say, marketing automation, you will have people with low-cost niche solutions, selling to you the concept of a 'quick and dirty' implementation. Buy us, we are low cost, get some quick wins and prove it out, then after a couple of years, because it's cloud, just turn it off. Whereas other salespeople will be saying that you need to look at this from a strategic point of view and small niche product is a waste of time and money; you can start small with us, but this is a 10-year application relationship.

When you add to that everybody's personal wins and political capital they may or may not want to spend, business to business (B2B) decisions are difficult and often just never happen as people are just too confused.

The art of closing is dead

Alex Low (https://www.linkedin.com/in/alexanderlow/) tells the story of how he went to purchase a car. He had configured the car online and all he needed from the Volkswagen (VW) salesman was to agree a price on the new one and a part exchange on the old one. What we are finding (certainly in Europe) is that you no longer need to close buyers, but empower them. However, the VW salesman assumed Low was at the start of the buying process and his rigid sales process forced Low to start from the beginning. Low walked out and purchased his car elsewhere.

More and more (there are exceptions which I will explain in a moment), prospects expect help and guidance from an expert and not the ABC – Always Be Closing – fantasy.

When people are researching online they are doing it in 'salesperson avoidance mode'; none of us likes to be sold to and the internet empowers us to do research in the comfort of our own home, or on the train into work. It is only when we know what we want and we are ready to buy that we might make contact with a salesperson. So we find today that clients don't want to be closed with force, they don't need to be. Our role as salespeople has changed to one of empowering them to buy.

Is sales dead or just sick?

As you can see from the above, while sales might not be dead it is on its sick bed. Buyers can and will bypass us and, while we cover it in the conclusion but not in the body of this book, artificial intelligence seems to be replacing us and our 'natural reaction' to sell seems to actually lose us deals rather than win them.

There are ways we can tackle this:

1 Assume that nothing has changed. In 2017 the US and Australia seemed to be in a pitched battle on LinkedIn and social media between 'cold callers' who said everything above hasn't happened and the 'social sellers' that recognized the world has changed. (The irony isn't lost on us that this battle takes place ON social media.) Cold callers live in this fantasy world, where you can call C-level people, interrupt them, pitch your product and service and you (a stranger) will be invited over for a coffee, where you will do a demo (demonstration).

2 Be manipulative. We have all been in a situation where we have been phoned or found ourselves in a situation where a salesperson has contacted us with a script and there can only be one answer. For many people, the instinctive reactions can often be either rude, disruptive or to buy. In fact, a whole industry has been created on how you can manipulatively get information on buyers (we talk about this later in the book). It might increase your open rates, but does it increase your sales?

3 Recognize that the world has changed and tackle this head-on.

But has sales actually changed?

Often we find that when we talk about social selling, salespeople think it will replace them. Forrester's 2015 report (Hora *et al*, 2015) states that 22 per cent of salespeople will be replaced. They talk about how search engines may replace salespeople, and in fact from the examples above, of transactional products that can be sold via self-service on the internet, why not?

But salespeople will always need to do what they do best:

1 Write compelling management summaries for Requests for Proposals (RFPs) and Invitations to Tender (ITTs).

2 Take complex solutions and present them in terms that everybody can understand.

3 Build rapport and relationships across an organization; later on in the book we talk about Account-Based Marketing (ABM), which should really be called Account-Based Sales (ABS) or, to go along with the title of this book, Account-Based Smarketing (ABS).

4 Muster the resources in your organization to help you work on sales. In all the organizations we have ever worked with, the best salespeople used the most resource. In fact, everybody wanted to work with the best salespeople as we all wanted to be associated with success. Success breeds success after all.

As you can see, the salesperson is going nowhere, but what about the future of sales?

In Tim's book *Social Selling: Techniques to influence buyers and changemakers*, co-authored alongside Matt Reynolds (2015), he writes about the challenges in the internet age, but he also writes about what the salesperson can do to support and help the modern buyer. This book is about the merger of sales and marketing so we don't intend to go into that in too much detail, but we recommend Tim's book as further reading. The world does not need another book on personal branding!

As buyers we are looking for people to help us to buy

As we talked about above, buyers are going online for 57 per cent of the way through the buying process (CEB Research, 2016) and we all avoid salespeople. One thing we do is seek advice, seek help. For example, on Amazon, there is a correlation between book sales and the number of reviews. My partner is an avid eBay seller and she makes sure that she goes above and beyond the call of duty for the buyer to ensure they grant her a five-star product and service review. She does the 'right thing' for the buyer so they give her five stars. As buyers we look for third-party validation when we buy.

As an aside there is a new website, https://bravado.me, which allows salespeople to be rated by their customers in a similar way to eBay, Uber, Airbnb, etc. The idea here is that as part of any contact with a client, or where a salesperson moves jobs, they can position themselves as the top professionals they are. For example, if you have sold to the Finance Director of Google, how would the Finance Director of Facebook know that they should take your call and you could do a similar good job for them? Or if you moved roles, how would your new territory and clients know to love you as much as your previous customers and territory? We digress.

In the same way you will check out a buyer on eBay or a restaurant on TripAdvisor, buyers will check out salespeople on LinkedIn and other social media. Salespeople will therefore need a 'personal brand'. A personal brand is not telling people how good you are. Well it is, but not in an arrogant, self-serving way. We want to tell people how good we are at helping people, like you the buyer, with finding the right solution.

It is critical not to sell, as that will put buyers off

Personal branding is hard work and as we say, this book isn't about creating one. But it does help you get 'inbound' from buyers. That is, to make your social media profiles work for you, they need to create inbound, rather than just being static profiles filled in using directions found on an article on the internet, regardless of how good that article was.

Buyer empowerment

Once the buyer makes contact with you it's then all about you empowering them to buy (rather than closing). Sellers need to understand that buyers will check them out on social media and then jump to a conclusion. Sellers that have an online brand that is just a CV (people tend to use LinkedIn in this way just to get another job, and it can make them look like a spammer) will find they are avoided, limiting the amount of inbound that they might get. We often get asked on social selling projects, 'we have sent multiple InMails on LinkedIn and nothing has happened'. This is pretty common where the seller's profile looks like they will you give a sales pitch or are a spammer. Why would anybody accept an InMail when they think they will get a sales pitch?

Salespeople now own the brand

The problem (for companies) with personal brands and buyer empowerment is that the employees become the brand. As we discuss in the next chapter in detail, in fact nobody cares about corporate branding anymore. Advertising and corporate messages have just become noise. Every company being 'number one', 'the best' all seems to be like an immaculate conception. In addition to that, there is the dysfunction we have discussed above in the buying process and the fact that social sellers have woken up to the fact that they can attract buyers, empower them and turn them into revenue ahead of the competition. There is an old sales quote that 'people buy people' or, as Bryan Kramer (http://bryankramer.com/) says in his 2014 book *There is no B2B and B2C*, the world is 'H2H – Human to Human'.

The ultimate sales strategy?

At a recent training session, I asked my students, if they had endless resources, what would be the 'ultimate sales strategy?' While I asked them slightly 'tongue in cheek', my students agreed their 'ultimate sales strategy' would be to take each of their customers out for lunch every day. During that time they could talk to their customers about their products and services. It would be the perfect sell. Every day sitting in front of their customers. I agree, they would certainly have their customers' 'attention' or be front of mind (FoM), as people say in digital marketing.

So why don't we do this?

It was quickly explained to me that this sales strategy does not scale; I was also reminded it wouldn't be good for our waistlines either. So when I suggested that this was possible, you can be 'front of mind' (FoM) with all your customers every day, and in fact 500 million business professionals worldwide, they wanted to know how. Of course there were other suggestions. Like phone them up every day – we agreed this might annoy them – or send them e-mails every day, again, maybe annoying. One student said he was once told by a customer, 'Look, we will buy your product, now stop calling us'. He wore his 'tenacity' badge with pride. We all agreed this seemed to work, but seemed risky short-term thinking.

Let's use advertising to get FoM of customers and prospects?

The next suggestion from my students was to buy ads (Google, Facebook, LinkedIn, etc).

So I asked the group, 'who today has been onto social media?' Everybody put their hand up. Next I asked, 'who today has been looking at adverts?' No hands went up. Why? We are on social media because we want to be there. If you are buying ads, it would seem that nobody is looking to read them.

How to get FoM with my customers, at scale?

So how do you get in front of your customers every day (in a way that scales) and not put on a pound in weight? Simple. Post something every day on LinkedIn and social media. You are probably thinking, 'So what, who cares what I post?' Think about when you page through your LinkedIn feed; you know who's boring and who's interesting. Yes?

Those people that are posting 'corporate twaddle': is your network really talking about some new supplier-focused, white paper? Of course they are not. We all laugh, shake our heads and think why are those poor salespeople and marketers stuck in the 1980s? So what do you think your customers are thinking? The same: 'Why do they keep posting all that corporate rubbish?' For your customer there is only one person that matters and it's them. For some this may come as a shock, but they don't care about you, your company or your products. So what can you do to be different and for your customer to actually look out for you in their social media feed?

Conclusion: be the light – you are what you post

Regardless of who you are as a reader – a business leader, salesperson or marketer – your social media profiles are there for everybody to see 365 days, 52 weeks a year, 7 days a week. People judge you and are jumping to conclusions based on your profile and by what you do or do not post. They judge you if you're boring, interesting, funny, helpful, honest, understand their industry, understand their business issues, seem trustworthy, will help out if their project goes wrong.

This book isn't about what good social media profiles look like, but by getting good at posting interesting, insightful 'stuff', telling people something they don't know, you will be front of mind (FoM) to all your customers, prospects and competitors' customers every day.

We are all now modern buyers; we all research things on the internet and we all avoid being pitched to, so why, as soon as we sit at our desks, do we think it is a good idea?

As we describe in this book, many of the tactics we have used in the past are either failing or just don't work anymore. There has to be a new way of work. In the next chapter we get into the detail of how you can bring sales and marketing together practically to make an impactful change.

Questions to ask yourself

1 Are you still selling the way you did pre the internet?

2 Are you selling the way you hate to buy?

3 Imagine yourself as a buyer; if you wanted to buy what you sell, could you find engaging and educational content online that you would want to read?

4 Are your salespeople using the internet to position themselves so that buyers see them as the solution to their problems?

5 How much inbound do your salespeople get on a daily basis?

References

Barnes, H (2016) 94% = Enterprise buying teams that have abandoned a buying effort with no decision (in the past 2 years), *Gartner Network Blog*. Available at: https://blogs.gartner.com/hank-barnes/2016/09/20/94-enterprise-buying-teams-that-have-abandoned-a-buying-effort-with-no-decision-in-the-past-2-years/ [Last accessed 25 May 2018]

CEB Research (2016) The revolution in B2B buying (CEB is now Gartner). Available at: https://www.cebglobal.com/sales-service/sales/b2b-revolution.html [Last accessed 25 May 2018]

Godin, S (1999) *Permission Marketing: Turning strangers into friends and friends into customers*, Simon & Schuster, London

Google Docs (nd) For a full list of the Martech 5,000 see this Google spreadsheet: https://docs.google.com/spreadsheets/u/2/d/1sgmWCLerELolXlHHMFHdxTWvBLIfmNrKTrlbz0vBW4E/pubhtml [Last accessed 25 May 2018]

Hora, A *et al* (2015) US B2B eCommerce Forecast: 2015 to 2020, *Forrester*. Available at: https://www.forrester.com/report/US+B2B+eCommerce+Forecast+2015+To+2020/-/E-RES115957 [Last accessed 25 May 2018]

Hughes, T and Reynolds, M (2015) *Social Selling: Techniques to influence buyers and changemakers*, Kogan Page, London

Kramer, B (2014) *There is no B2B and B2C: It's Human to Human #H2H*. Available at: http://bryankramer.com/pages/books/ [Last accessed 25 May 2018]

Peppers, D and Rogers, M (1999) *The One to One Fieldbook*, Crown Business, New York

Spenner, P and Schmidt, K (2015) Two numbers you should care about, *CEB Blogs*. Available at: https://www.cebglobal.com/blogs/b2b-sales-and-marketing-two-numbers-you-should-care-about/ [Last accessed 25 May 2018]

So where are customers today? 03

Get closer than ever to your customers. So close that you tell them what they need well before they realize it themselves.
STEVE JOBS

In this chapter we will talk about where customers were in the past, the barriers they built to block the messages of both marketers and salespeople, and where they are today in the internet, mobile, social media age we live in today. We will discuss how buying behaviours have changed and how marketers can win a prospective customer's trust. We will also talk about how buyers (even senior executives) will listen to you, the mistakes people often make on social media, as well as the secrets to marketing and selling today.

Once upon a time, the only way that customers found out about a company's products and services was by being interrupted by the company.

The birth of marketing

Leo Burnett was a leading marketer in the 1930s who decided that consumers needed to be 'touched' by brands, 'touched' being a metaphor for being interrupted or told about a product or service.

In a world without the internet, consumers were inundated with advertisements (as this was the only way to get people's attention) in newspapers, on the television, everywhere. Advertising agencies measured adverts by 'eyeballs'; this is a theoretical maximum number of people that could see your advert.

Old-school marketing

If your newspaper had a circulation of 60,000 people and research showed that an average of 1.5 people saw each copy of the paper, then it stands to reason that 90,000 people could see your advert. The fact that people may and probably do ignore adverts or don't want to be interrupted means that getting in front of consumers gets more and more difficult with time.

In fact, the laws of Leo Burnett were simple. The more you spent on advertising, the more you told people about your product, the more you interrupted them, the more likely people would buy. This whole attitude was demonstrated in the television show *Mad Men*.

Advertising and brochures

Advertisements created icons. We can all remember an advertising slogan from our childhood. Or visual icons such as the 'Marlborough Man', the cowboy riding in the desert smoking cigarettes, who idealized the notion that smoking was a wonderful thing. We all now know that smoking causes cancer, but regardless of if we smoke or not many of us bought into the 'cowboy notion'.

When I was in my early teens I was into cars. I wanted to know all about them and I would write to car companies, pretending to be in the market for one of their cars and ask for a brochure. I'm sure many companies just thought it was 'some kid' and would send me the brochure and forget about it. The letters were handwritten and on scrappy bits of paper, so I'm sure many people didn't think I was really looking for a car. But imagine my parents' surprise when a car company rang up and asked for 'Mr Hughes'; my father answered, 'Yes, Mr Hughes speaking'. The car salesman then asked if that was Mr Tim Hughes and asked about the car test drive. My father pointed out I was only 12.

Don't forget, this was before the internet. The only way I could get more information was via trade shows (I recall going to a car show and getting bags of brochures) or by writing away.

How marketing controlled the message

These brochures (as well as the advertisements) were written by marketing departments and told you how amazing the cars were. I remember that the tag line for the Ford Sierra (the newly released replacement for the Ford Cortina) was 'man and machine in perfect harmony'. Being 12 at the time, I'm not sure if grown-ups believed this (although I must admit at 12 I was a little cynical) but nonetheless if Ford was telling me this, surely they knew better than me and it must be right? Reading this back, I realize this makes me look pretty naive and maybe I was. But then returning through the eyes of a 52-year-old, everyone has 20:20 hindsight!

I'm sure you are smiling and thinking, no way; even today, in the artificial intelligence world we still don't have man and machine in total harmony. And I agree.

But ever since the beginning of time, we the consumer have been bombarded with messages that products are the best, a company is number one, the company is the largest. One recruitment company told me they were the best as they had 'the largest square footage of office'. They were deadly serious, but quite how this size of your offices correlates to a measure of quality I don't know. They, however, made that connection.

If you are aware of a company that markets itself by saying they are the number two best company in the world, please contact us and let us know.

But the point is that we were sold to through advertisements and marketing materials such as brochures and, regardless of if we agreed or not, people purchased. More importantly, there was nowhere else to find information. Look at today; we can go online and configure cars: colour, interior, wheel trims. We can see a 3D image on our laptops, while we watch the X-Factor and nearly buy the car, apart from the fact that car companies force us to talk to their salespeople.

How marketing lost control

We have all been worn down by this, in fact I would say it's become noise. Consumers can now access information across multiple channels.

Social media (Facebook, LinkedIn, Twitter, Reddit, Pinterest, WeChat, YouTube, etc) and the internet are great sources of information.

Many customers turn to them for information as well as search engines such as Google or Bing, and we may start a customer journey already in the place where we know we will want to buy, such as Amazon etc. For example, if you want to buy a CD or a book you may well turn to Amazon rather than Google.

Social media and search engines are 'open networks' where we can search for information on products and services and the information we can find is pretty endless. The company brochure (while being online) is probably the last place we go. We look for reviews or write-ups. These can be by ordinary members of the public or third-party reviews from, maybe, influencers.

If Hilton Hotels tell you they have the best hotel in Florida you may believe them; if I tell you the Hilton in Florida is the best and you are my friend, then you are more likely to book it for a stay. If corporate marketing tell us they have the best products in the world, as consumers we will tune out as everybody says that; if the employees tell you they work for the best company in the world you may give them the benefit of the doubt (even though they might be biased). But if they write a blog that is well structured, passionate and insightful, you will probably believe them and possibly share it through your network, thus amplifying the message.

How many of us have checked out a restaurant based on third-party reviews or purchased a book from Amazon because of the reviews? You may not know any of the reviewers but having the endorsements creates a 'halo' effect that supports your buying decision. Corporate marketing is in difficulty as we tune the generic 'brand messages' (or perhaps 'bland messages') out.

Going where marketing fears to tread

Dark social (which isn't as sinister as it sounds) is WhatsApp groups, Facebook groups, LinkedIn groups, Slack groups, Yammer groups, etc.

Before we go any further, we'd better define what we mean by 'dark social'. This isn't an area where cybercriminals hang out. Well they might (we all need to be careful online), but dark social means areas closed off to some non-members. So rather than a social network where you can track how the content is shared and amplified, with dark social, as a marketer, you cannot.

Private social networks on WhatsApp, Facebook, Slack, etc are where people may be there by invite only, so you can be far more 'open' with people in terms of buying intention or seeking advice on a future purchase.

Simplistically, many families have WhatsApp groups and can see the power of co-operation or crowdsourcing in terms of babysitting, being picked up from the shopping mall, or general discussions around friends and family as a group. These groups are also used for spreading ideas. In the last UK General Election, both parties used them as a way of spreading messages that people could then share on social media. For example, the Labour Party provided party slogans that could be disseminated through communities of activists onto social media, increasing the amplification and also making sure that the messages seemed to come from ordinary people, rather than a political machine.

Buyers now focus on what interests them

With access to the internet and social networks, buyers are able to seek out the products and services that they want, regardless of how niche they are, without the need to contact a company or a salesperson. In fact, we will actively avoid talking with corporations, companies and salespeople, as they will sell to us and we all hate being sold to.

A friend of ours recently purchased a car. They went online and decided which car, model and make they wanted. The purchaser also went onto social media (Facebook) and asked their network for advice. What did people think of the car choice and where did they think she should buy it from?

This literally crowdsourced their decision, using her friends and family as 'influencers' on the final decision. In the end she purchased the car from a car dealer that was not the closest one as the reviews and discussion on social media advised her not to buy from the local dealer.

The marketer's nightmare

What I've outlined is every marketer and salesperson's nightmare. People can make decisions for (maybe) competitors' products using data on the internet and comments from families and friends. But do they?

Buyers are now in control of the buying process

According to CEB, now part of Gartner, buyers are now 57 per cent of the way through the buying process by the time they contact a company to seek any information and when they contact a company they won't be asking for a brochure (CEB Research, 2016).

I'm not saying that this is exactly 57 per cent; you might reach out earlier, or in the car example above, when you have researched and configured it online you might be 80 or 90 per cent of the way through the buying process. I've had people come to me and say, 'We have seen you on YouTube, please can we book you to speak at our sales conference?' The discussion then is only about price and whether I'm available.

In addition to the 57 per cent figure is the 37 per cent discussed in Chapter 2 (Spenner and Schmidt, 2015). With buyers in control they are researching the products and services they want to buy on the internet and social media. They are doing this by reviewing content such as articles, reviews, blogs, videos, webinars. They are also turning to influencers, the same way you might read reviews on Amazon, Airbnb, eBay, etc.

(Influencers could be Gartner, PWC, KPMG, Accenture, known figures such as Ted Rubin, Brian Solis or the authors of this book, as well as colleagues or family and friends as in the example above.)

The 37 per cent figure comes from the review process. If we are searching for a holiday, for example we might want to go to Spain. We can research the hotels and flights online, we can look up and check the reviews. We can also get a feeling for our itinerary which could be scuba diving, mountain biking, horse riding or even sitting on the beach. We no longer need to go through a single holiday company, but can deal with the various providers direct. Right down to the ability to book a seat at the surf shack on the beach.

We are, on average, 37 per cent through the buying process when we understand our requirements. If you haven't influenced the buyer by this stage you are not on the shortlist. More on this later.

The exposition of social media

Let's look at the 'Hootsuite' and 'We are Social' research for August 2017 (Kemp, 2017).

From an internet perspective, we have reached a tipping point; 51 per cent of the world's population, 3.819 billion people, now have access to the world wide web. Forty per cent of the global population, 3.028 billion are now on social media, with 2.780 billion, which is 37 per cent of the world's population, being active. In the three months previous to writing, 121 million people joined social media. Now many people reading this in the West may think that social media growth has stopped or slowed up, but in fact it's growing exponentially. Somebody said to me the other day, 'If they are not on social media, in my mind, they don't exist'. And they also said, 'If somebody isn't on social media, I don't trust them. What are they trying to hide?!'

Google and Facebook are investing in IT infrastructure in the areas without access to the internet so they can continue their user growth. Twitter have created a lite version to be used in Africa.

The future is... mobile

This has been driven by easier access to the internet across the world as well as the drive to use mobile as the platform of choice to access the internet, social media as well as apps and data services.

We did some training in Kuala Lumpur in December 2016 and asked the attendees to bring their laptops. Of the 12 students who attended the course three didn't have a laptop or mac: they accessed everything through mobile.

Using the same 'Hootsuite' and 'We are Social' research for August 2017, we learn that 650,000 people sign up to mobile... every day. The average data used by a mobile every month is 2.3 gigabytes. This is a 70 per cent increase on the previous year.

From social media to gaming and app usage, for example online banking, etc, mobile is the single most important device (or tool) for two-thirds of the world's population.

How buyer behaviour has changed

For this mobile generation the buying process has changed. We might start our buying process online and then end up in a shop or 'showroom'. Or we might be starting in a shop and then end up online. Either way the internet is part of the buying process. This could be searching for the best products or prices online or scanning codes while we are in a shop to see if we can buy the product at a cheaper price, maybe in another shop or online. In the business-to-business (B2B) world we have seen the internet influence the buying processes throughout the buyer journey and across 100 per cent of the pipeline.

In future chapters we talk about 'intent' data and how as a business you should be using this in your Smarketing organization.

The buyer owns the buying process, not the seller

None of us like being sold or marketed to. Fact. Added to the technology explosion and massive take-up of social media and mobile is the fact that in society we avoid salespeople and tune out corporate marketing messages.

As we mentioned above, in the past, 'touching' a client was the only way to sell our goods. It was the only way people could find out about our goods or services. The only way this could be achieved was through interruption so I would interrupt what you're doing with my message. You are in the middle of working on a massive spreadsheet calculation and you don't want to be disturbed by the phone ringing and it's a salesman trying to sell you something. Or you get to an important part of a film and the adverts come on. Which of course you fast-forward through. We all have the power of the internet at our fingertips and we use that. As mentioned previously in the chapter, we don't believe adverts as they all just tell us that the company is the best or the fastest and it all turns into noise.

The rise of the gatekeeper

What is a gatekeeper? A gatekeeper can be a person such as a secretary, personal assistant, or answerphone, voicemail, spam filter, ad blocker, anything that places a barrier between the salesperson and the prospective customer. The gatekeeper's role has grown over the years as people have less and less time, or are more and more busy, and put barriers in place so they are not bothered/interrupted by salespeople. Talking with a number of secretaries, the average business leader gets 20 to 50 cold calls a day. Most if not all of these are turned away by secretaries.

In fact, a whole industry has grown up called 'sales hacking', with hints and tips to get round these barriers, such as how to find executives' e-mail addresses, mobile numbers or simply knowing to call at 8 am when the personal assistant hasn't arrived at work yet.

As the barriers increase, the ability to get through becomes less and less. I can recall when you needed to make 50 calls a day to get the requisite number of meetings, but there has been 'cold-calling inflation' over the last few years, with cold callers needing to make 80, 100 or 120 calls a day. Companies employ dialer software, so the salesperson does not need to dial; as they finish one call, they are offered the next person to try and get through to. Like a factory.

In fact, we think that the idea today that somebody (whom you don't know) can call upon somebody, pitch about products and services and persuade the senior executive to agree to a meeting is utter fantasy. We do see on LinkedIn people saying cold calling works, but certainly as the size of the contract increases and the time to buy increases the effectiveness of cold calling decreases.

Buyer empowerment

When I started selling 25 years ago sales was so much simpler. You listened to a client's business requirements, you matched back your product and services. You probed for your unique selling points (USPs) and got the client to say these were the priorities locking the competition out. But in reality, clients would still need to look at three suppliers as the procurement department needed to show they were getting the best price. You would guide the client through the different stages of the procurement as you knew the steps and they didn't.

That has all changed. In many cases now (that we come across) clients have completed the buying process online. They have already decided what they want.

In the film *Glengarry Glenn Ross* (YouTube, 2007) a young Alec Baldwin gave the famous speech about 'ABC – Always Be Closing'. In the past, salespeople were in control. In the film, the salespeople call upon prospects and feed them a line that they are in the area and have a special deal for them; or, in the case of Ricky Roma (the part played by Al Pacino) the salesperson gets the unsuspecting prospect slowly drunk in a bar, pounces with the sales pitch and closes for the signature.

The problem for salespeople today is that the buyer is no longer naive, and in fact they undertake part if not all of their purchasing process online, away from the sight of the salesperson. By the time the salesperson is approached, the prospect will already know about the product or service, the competition. They will have read price lists, spoken to and got third-party reviews from colleagues and watched videos on YouTube. The modern buyer is highly sophisticated and woe betide the salesman that tries to close. Buyers hate being sold to and run a mile.

The salesperson of today needs to empower the buyer to buy. The buyer, with all that research online, is probably often confused or at least needs help and guidance and they will probably close themselves.

If you think about it, we all go online and research the products we buy, from cars to multimillion enterprise systems. In fact, the higher the value the more likely we are to go online and research.

Buyers are not just selecting but also deselecting

Don't forget that buyers also de-select shortlists online just as much as they select. According to the CEB research quoted above they are 37 per cent of the way through the buying process when they know or understand what it is they want to buy. Fifty-seven per cent of the way through the buying process, they are pretty sure, which is when they make contact or stop being in salesperson avoidance mode.

The exceptions are where salespeople buy from salespeople or when you are going for a sales job and as salespeople live in a 'bubble' where we have to close, as there is an expectation. For example, When we closed our recent reseller agreement with our new partner in Canada, we closed them. We were negotiating with another salesperson and he expected it. Call it old fashioned I guess.

How does a modern marketer/ salesperson sell?

They don't, or not as they have done in the past. So what is the secret?

While people buy from people, for sure, the people we will buy from are our family and friends. We are 71 per cent more likely to buy from a referral or a review (Heinz Marketing, 2015). It helps if we know the person but as TripAdvisor and Amazon show, it might not be so. This means that for the salesperson to sell or the marketer to market today, they need to build trust with the buyer. The buyer needs to see that the buying transaction is worthwhile. That is, there is some 'value' exchange between the buyer and seller.

One of the ways that a salesperson can create trust is to set themselves up as an expert. Salespeople have always been experts, that is, we know more than our buyers. As we discussed above, we know that the modern buyer is looking for help and advice having completed research online. If a salesperson sets himself or herself up as an expert via a personal brand online, then the buyer might approach the expert for help. Please don't underestimate the modern buyer; don't forget that the modern buyer is savvy. If they think for a second that you are pitching or it looks like you are not legitimate, you will be dropped.

How does the modern seller present himself or herself as the solution to a buyer's problem?

Personal brands enable salespeople to be experts. They are not there to make out you are something you are not, or a narcissist. This book isn't about how to create a personal brand. In summary it's about presenting yourself on social media, so that when a buyer finds you they jump to the conclusion you are the solution to their problem. Also, when we say jump to the conclusion, you have to be authentic and let's remember, people buy from people and not salespeople drowning in corporate speak and jargon.

One-to-one marketing

While marketers today talk about being 'hyper-personalized' there is nothing like being marketed to one-to-one. This is nothing new, Seth Godin in *Permission Marketing* and Don Peppers and Martha Rodgers in *The One to One Fieldbook* all talked of a day where people could know enough about us that we could receive a totally focused approach.

This is very different from the old days of 'spray and pray' cold calling. There is now enough detail about us online for people to offer a totally focused approach to our wants and needs. You can have the best-written copy, with the best images all written by the best agency in the world, but if you spell my name wrong, it's going to get deleted.

Better still, with buyers researching online and coming to decisions online, an 'inbound' marketing strategy is very common, where the need for outreach is superseded by buyers finding you and seeking your expertise, either directly by asking questions of our networks (Who would you recommend to undertake a piece of work?) or a referral.

The value exchange

While the term 'value' tends to be overused and often misunderstood, in the buying process, there is an exchange, not just of money for goods or services, but also of a buyer swapping time (something we don't have a lot of) and getting something in return. Like a teacher, a mentor or a friend. If I'm going to buy something of 'significant' value, I'm going to make sure that if I don't know about the subject, the person that guides, helps, let's me know where I might fail, is more likely to be my friend and therefore I'm more likely to buy from them.

How to not alienate the buyer

The seller must, when engaging with the buyer, be careful not to alienate them. This is less about showing people how much we know, like we did in the past, and more about understanding how much the buyer knows. This enables you to make the judgement as to where the buyer is in their journey. It enables the seller to empower the buyer to buy.

Jargon or talking using a company's internal words are classic ways to alienate a buyer. For example, in the world of accounting software, while we may not know what it does, we probably all know what an accountant is and therefore understand that an accountant may use accounting software. Software suppliers, in the need to give everything a three-letter acronym (TLA), have come up with the term ERP – Enterprise Resource Planning. Same thing as accounting software but a far grander title, don't you agree?

'I'm an ERP salesperson' sounds grander than 'I'm an accounting software salesperson'. Well, suppliers think so. This is all very well except customers know what accounting is but don't know what ERP is. We recall a company that had registered their software in a government catalogue (as ERP) and customers complained they could never find the products. They were searching for accounting software.

'Equal to equal' selling

Selling involves equals talking to equals, that is, it needs to be peer-to-peer selling. That means you need a director talking to a director. It's often called multi-level selling. How does this work? The salesperson in the past would cold outreach an account and while they would or should sell at the highest level, the problem was often that senior executives would not talk to 'ordinary salespeople' so you were pushed down the hierarchy to somebody with a similar rank to you.

That's where you would involve your manager in the sale on the basis that he or she would be a director and they could engage and build a relationship with their peer. In the world of social media, hierarchies have flattened, and in fact in many places been eliminated. All good news for the 'average salesperson'. The secret? Senior executives will talk with thought leaders.

If we take the online personal brand a step further, with salespeople and marketers becoming thought leaders, senior executives will not only take cold outreach from them, they will actively seek them out. For example, we have contacted a managing director of a multi-billion-dollar organization via a cold outreach using a social network on a Thursday and had a meeting with him, his marketing director and head of public relations (PR) on the following Tuesday.

In fact, he employed us to roll out a social selling programme for him and he cited this at the kick-off meeting with his sales team as to why social selling worked and cold calling didn't. He in fact blocked all cold outreach and he said it offered him no value.

Often salespeople are told to give prospects and customers 'insight' or to 'tell them something they don't know' and this is taken to the nth degree by being a thought leader as a salesperson or marketer. And I'm not saying that is easy. But by having that level or position on social will alleviate the problem of both marketing inbound and cold outreach in the modern social world.

Conclusion

In this chapter we have covered how, through the advent of the internet, the buying process has changed. We have all gone onto the internet and researched products and services we want to buy. Slowly companies and salespeople are waking up to this disruption to the marketing and selling process. We have seen the introduction of social selling and digital marketing as reactions to this. Many of these changes have been at a micro level; individuals and departments, mostly tactics and incremental change. But the change isn't enough. In the next chapter we will discuss how the sales and marketing departments need to start to transform and how companies can start looking from a strategic and macro level to change company strategy.

Questions to ask yourself

1 Is your company educating the internet-empowered customer with insightful and educational content, blogs and videos along 100 per cent of the buying process?

2 Have you empowered your employees to talk, post and blog about the amazing opportunity working for your company provides, tapping into the power of their passion?

3 If you get a prospective customer contact do you assume they are at the start of a buying process or part-way through? Are your marketing and sales processes agile so that you don't make assumptions?

4 Is your marketing hyper-personalized or one-to-one personalized?

5 Are your marketing, sales and employees 'adding value' to your prospects and customers?

References

CEB Research (2016) The revolution in B2B buying (CEB is now Gartner). Available at: https://www.cebglobal.com/sales-service/sales/b2b-revolution.html [Last accessed 25 May 2018]

Godin, S (1999) *Permission Marketing: Turning strangers into friends and friends into customers*, Simon & Schuster, London

Heinz Marketing (2015) What you should know about B2B referrals (but probably don't), *Heinz Marketing*. Available at: https://www.heinzmarketing.com/2015/12/new-research-formal-referral-programs-lead-to-higher-sales-faster-deals/ [Last accessed 25 May 2018]

Kemp, S (2017) Hootsuite & We Are Social 2017 research, in Social media users surge past 3 billion, *LinkedIn*. Available at: https://www.linkedin.com/pulse/social-media-users-surge-past-3-billion-simon-kemp/ [Last accessed 25 May 2018]

Peppers, D and Rogers, M (1999) *The One to One Fieldbook,* Crown Business, New York

Spenner, P and Schmidt, K (2015) Two numbers you should care about, *CEB Blogs*. Available at: https://www.cebglobal.com/blogs/b2b-sales-and-marketing-two-numbers-you-should-care-about/ [Last accessed 25 May 2018]

YouTube (2007) Alec Baldwin Glengarry Glenn Ross always be closing full speech. Available at: https://youtu.be/Q4PE2hSqVnk [Last accessed 18 June 2018]

Sales and marketing departments of the future

04

Every contact we have with a customer influences whether or not they'll come back. We have to be great every time or we'll lose them.
KEVIN STIRTZ

In this chapter we switch from the why to the how of implementing Smarketing, and introduce a number of new concepts and terminology. As we have seen from the previous chapters, the internet is driving change and sales and marketing need to react. It would be wrong for us to say 'react or die', but we are seeing that companies still using legacy sales and marketing methods are falling behind.

In this chapter we cover the need for a merger of the sales director and marketing director roles; how there needs to be the creation of a new, joined-up sales and marketing language; the need to treat the sales pipeline as a single process with no hand-off between sales and marketing; and an introduction to account-based techniques enabling companies to engage with new buyer trends based on the fact that buyers buy in groups, teams or organizations, rather than the legacy sales and marketing methods that assumed a one-to-one engagement.

Why do we need to change?

As discussed in the chapters so far, most organizations have separated sales and marketing functions based on the skills and expertise of each discipline, with experienced domain experts running each function. This may seem highly logical and a sensible way to allow the autonomy needed for each discipline to thrive. It is clear that the skills and approaches of sales and marketing are not the same and therefore separated management and leadership can seem to be the right option, allowing both departments to build their strategies, processes and execution to achieve their objectives based on their resources and skills.

Rhiannon Prothero – Marketing Director UK & Ireland, SAP

Often in large enterprises central corporate marketing can have a very clear view of what they think the regions should be supporting and in some cases that neatly lines up with the business and what they need, but where that doesn't line up, who wins? In my view it's the customer.

If ever we come up against that, when we've got a product-specific marketing objective but actually in region, we've said that we want to be customer-centric, who wins? Well, that's our choice and ultimately that's up to me to decide and I will always go with 'the customer wins' in this particular challenge.

However, when we look closely at this existing norm it becomes apparent that much closer alignment in the future becomes more compelling if organizations are to be truly successful. In an increasingly competitive global environment, companies need their marketing and sales teams more than ever to drive their competitive edge as buyers become aware faster via the internet, not just traditional word of mouth. All this against the backdrop of immense digital noise that prevents all but the most well-funded brands from gaining any differentiation with buyers. In the future this business will be even more challenged and as such something needs to change to allow an organization to use its resources more effectively.

There are many examples in the press on a regular basis of organizations with big names that have failed. The reasons for these failures are varied, culminating in some form of financial failure that brings the entity down. But well before this it is possible to see the failings arising in how the organization engages its customers and therefore starts to lose its customer base and ultimately fails. The more siloed organizations are, the less they are able to understand and have the full picture of what is driving changes in their business.

Some major brands like Blockbuster in the United States, Schlecker in Germany and MG Rover in the UK all failed due to a lack of understanding of the desires of their customers. Attempts to adapt failed as the departments within these organizations did not have the full picture and any changes were not radical enough. One example of this is the troubled story of Rover Group and subsequently MG Rover, which, over the course of five years had its market share cut by three-quarters, meaning that in 10 years the broader brand reduced its sales by 90 per cent from the 1996 figure to the number in the year before its ultimate demise under the MG Rover brand.

Where to start on the reasons why this business failed? There are many, but underpinning all of this at the start of the company's trouble was its inability to understand the customer's needs and the failure to deliver a product that was desirable in the market. A trade union review in 2000 put it perfectly: 'Rover cars: The problem is selling them'. The full story and the many additional reasons for its collapse are covered in the book *End of the Road: The true story of the downfall of Rover* (Brady and Mullins, 2005) for those readers wanting to understand more and some of the intricacies that can cause a business to fail. For any major business to become so disconnected from the customers who are so critical to its survival is one of the clear reasons why sales and marketing need to join. In a world where the pace of change is ultra-fast, with instant global communication, any business has to adopt a Smarketing approach in how it operates to safeguard against loss of market share, detachment from the customer and potential collapse.

Our future is Smarketing

Sales and marketing a single unified leader – the Chief Smarketing Officer (CSO)

We see that a clear way to increase the effectiveness of a modern business is to join the two departments of sales and marketing and disregard the historical siloed approach to customer engagement and management. We will cover in more detail the benefits of doing this but the key objective is to increase the quality of the customer experience by aligning the business across the whole customer engagement cycle. The first step of this unification is to have a single leader for these two departments, which might be an evolution from co-locating the roles but you should have one executive with all of marketing and sales reporting to them. This role of Chief Smarketing Officer (CSO) can then become the guide and inspiration for the unification throughout these two departments. The way that a company then structures its teams will vary hugely depending on the business objectives, but it should be the premise of this single leader to define this structure to bridge any historical gaps between sales and marketing.

A key priority for this role which will be a driver to transforming the departments is to establish consistent reporting and KPIs around which the combined function should be structured and incentivized. This would not be a process of replacing historical KPIs such as web traffic at the top of the customer engagement funnel and won business at the bottom, but measuring them and reporting on them end to end. For a business to understand the full picture of its success in the market it needs this end-to-end view irrespective of what is measured or the steps in the process.

Coming back to the reasons why one should move to Smarketing, this is a clear and compelling reason that will give the board and other business decision makers the vision to steer the organization more effectively. Any CEO is always looking in detail at the financial results and the closed sales figures but do they look in detail at other indicators? In our experience, very rarely, and the larger the company the less this is the case as the financial figures become the key metric led by the CFO. Trusting the interpretation of these other figures to the individual business leaders builds an inherent lack of visibility for any business.

A CSO brings the full view to the boardroom and can complement the CFO more effectively to provide that complete picture of the other key metrics around customer engagement that actually give all the indicators on the fitness of a business. We cover the CSO in more detail in subsequent chapters but here are some of the traits that this person needs to be successful in this role.

Table 4.1 Traits of a Smarketing leader

Trait	Summary	Importance
Selling experience	Having run a commercial process end to end	Medium
Marketing execution	Delivered a marketing campaign or major event	Medium
Business strategy	Developed and adapted business plans through to execution	Very high
Financial management	Managed large fiscal sums both in terms of targets and also budgets	High
Change management	Led multifaceted complex change projects	Very high
Stakeholder management	Used to managing up and effectively communicating across departments	High

An example of this would be something simple like web traffic, where a drop in this correctly understood will indicate a drop in sales in future months. When you go to buy a car, how many times do you visit various manufacturer websites and use the building tools to create your ideal vehicle? You may do this many times over the course of your decision making and this is a vital indicator for the business of future sales. But at the board level are they really looking at the number of cars built on the web app as the most important metric of future sales? No, this simply does not happen. This information is entrusted to the marketing department who will no doubt be diligent in taking action to improve the traffic to this app, the experience in using the app and the follow-up e-mails, banner ads and other engagement tactics, but never anything more. They are not linking this to the sales teams or notifying the sales teams in dealerships that a reduction in their area means extra attention and service should be applied for any new person that enters that dealership. Here are some examples of the different metrics that are measured across sales and marketing and where the divide between sales and marketing often lies.

The traditional division between sales and marketing

As we will come to in subsequent chapters, the process for moving to Smarketing needs many different areas of change and focus to deliver the Smarketing department but a key issue that we wanted to highlight prior to that is the historical areas of handover between sales and marketing in the customer engagement process. You can see on the engagement funnel that this point of handover is shown in the transition from Business Qualified Lead (BQL) to Sales Qualified Lead (SQL). If you think of any organization there is always a point in the engagement with its customers where support and engagement moves from the marketing department to the sales department. This is the key point of focus for starting to change to becoming a Smarketing organization and the area that the CSO should have as their clear priority to address. The detail on where to start and how to do this is covered in Chapters 5 and 6 in more detail.

Note: MQL = Marketing Qualified Lead

What are MQL, BQL and SQL?

At this point it might be worth defining what MQL, BQL and SQL are. In the new world of sales and marketing working together, companies need to have a common language as to what a lead is. The example often used is that marketing runs a competition at an event, where if you drop your business card into a box you can win a bottle of champagne. These cards are then handed to salespeople back at the office as 'leads'. Sales then spend time following these leads up only to find the people just wanted to win a bottle of champagne and that there was no clear need for the offer that was actually being presented. To understand the need of the person being engaged there needs clarification of their requirements via some form of sales qualification, and offering the champagne did not do that; there is no Budget, Authority, Need or Timescale (BANT), to use one of the main sales qualification methods. Overall, while marketing will say it is all about awareness and branding and will enable sales to have a conversation and a reason to call, sales think this is a waste of time.

Figure 4.1 Engagement funnel

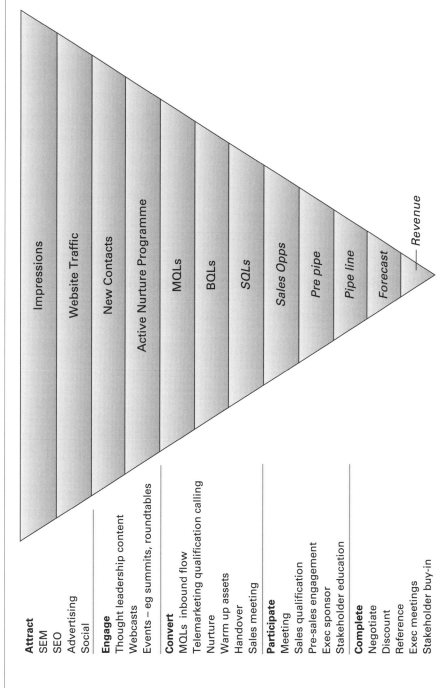

Attract
SEM
SEO
Advertising
Social

Engage
Thought leadership content
Webcasts
Events – eg summits, roundtables

Convert
MQLs inbound flow
Telemarketing qualification calling
Nurture
Warm up assets
Handover
Sales meeting

Participate
Meeting
Sales qualification
Pre-sales engagement
Exec sponsor
Stakeholder education

Complete
Negotiate
Discount
Reference
Exec meetings
Stakeholder buy-in

Impressions
Website Traffic
New Contacts
Active Nurture Programme
MQLs
BQLs
SQLs
Sales Opps
Pre pipe
Pipe line
Forecast
— *Revenue*

Therefore, in the brand-new world of sales and marketing there has to be a definition of what a lead is. A marketing qualified lead (MQL) is those business cards, or they can be names on a spreadsheet. Once somebody, often an internal salesperson, has made contact with the individual they run them through some sort of qualification process. BANT is the example above, but there are many more. They tend to filter people who put their business cards in the bowl just to win a bottle of champagne and those who may have had an actual interest. These are now business qualified leads (BQLs). The BQLs are then handed over to the salespeople and once accepted as qualified they become sales qualified leads (SQLs). Sometimes the whole process takes place in the CRM (customer relationship management) database, with many CRMs supporting it. Sometimes the SQL will be the first time that the lead is registered.

For Smarketing we need an ideal customer criteria

A key tenet of Smarketing is also to clearly document the right definition of the customer. Surprisingly this is something that can be incorrectly characterized in the engagement funnel for B2B companies and often comes from the historical implementation of CRM systems in the late 1990s and early 2000s.

This is where companies define the engagement cycle based on the lowest-level entity within their CRM system, which is a contact or individual, but the reality is that in B2B it is an organization that is being sold to. As such the whole engagement cycle and the systems that support it need to be focused on organizations, not individuals. This leads to a whole new characterization based on organization engagement, not contact engagement. As many technology solutions for managing customers are built for both B2C and B2B the contact-centricity of these systems is fundamental irrespective of your business.

An example would be where an intern is used to contact an organization in relation to a new purchase. This may well be a multi-million purchase, but it is seen by the buyer organization as a good project. The intern contacts a number of suppliers but they are not registered by the selling suppliers as being important so the lead (MQL) is not taken any further forward, or fails a qualification criteria at BQL stage, and again, is not taken any further.

As such this can be a challenge in setting the process to be more aligned to the company being sold to rather than the individual within it. However, as outlined in Chapter 6 this can be overcome by organizational alignment around the technology-enabled process elements and with the right reporting to drive the automation or decision making within the process of customer engagement.

A basic example of this would be the sale of lorries to a haulier. The manufacturer of the lorries picks up the first interest from an organization when its fleet manager engages via the website. This could be research, signing up for more information on a model or registering for an informative event run by the manufacturer. From this point the fleet manager will be placed into the CRM system, tracked and engaged based on the marketing process that the company has put in place. Once the fleet manager has carried out enough actions to become a marketing qualified suspect or lead they will then be engaged directly, possibly by a junior sales representative or telemarketing individual to qualify them further. At the relevant point they will be passed on to a sales rep who will offer more involved engagement, propose a solution and progress them to closure against other competitors.

As a basic outline of the engagement process these might seem like logical steps but this is forgetting that the manufacturer is actually selling to a company and the fleet manager is just its representative. In reality there are many more people involved in the buying process and these may only be engaged when the sales rep carries out a face-to-face meeting.

It is for this reason that the process needs to track this and engage at a company level, so bring together information from all contacts in the company, be it the CEO making a statement on the annual report about improving the energy efficiency of their fleet or the HR department advertising for talent managers due to high driver turnover which could be partly caused by old fleet stock. For a B2B-focused organization, engaging solely individuals is flawed; the process should be based on companies or entities, not individuals.

Building the processes to address these sorts of issues in the engagement cycle is a key driver for Smarketing and underpins why this is of direct relevance to the competitiveness and profitability of organizations.

How do we merge sales and marketing?

In many organizations, sales and marketing can be seen as 'chalk and cheese'; sales is focused on revenue, whereas marketing can be focused on creativity. That said, as we have talked about above, companies need to merge sales and marketing, not just because it is a good idea but because the market demands it and we need to respond to the buyer dysfunction powered by the internet.

Sales and marketing structure

Merging sales and marketing operations

To underpin a changed approach to customer engagement, support functions that were historically split need to become joined. Operations teams are a common example of split groups that clearly benefit from being joined. Marketing operations with a specialism in web stats, first- and third-party data analysis as well as generally being top of the engagement funnel statistics have always missed out on the benefit of analysis down the whole customer engagement funnel. Similarly, sales operations focused on productivity, progression and participation metrics lack the analysis in most cases of which types of opportunity will be most productive and require the most focus from a sales rep. Bringing these two groups together provides the incentive to look at factors across the entire engagement process providing opportunities for deeper insight but ultimately more focus. The analysis that joined-up operations can offer, if correctly organized, is immense and provides the complete view that is complementary to the CFO reporting to the board.

Merging sales and marketing execution

Again focus is the ultimate objective of the modern Smarketing department.

Additional approaches to structure should involve the joining of the marketing and sales execution. Interestingly marketing was historically not always directly aligned to sales or vice versa, with organizational structures often growing out of the demand for results from each siloed piece of the business.

As a business grows, the leadership within each area of the business will organize and request more staff based on the challenges and demands in front of them; the more siloed their view is, the less effectively they can build their departments. Apart from some of the usual organizational inefficiencies of duplication, this approach limits versatility. Another benefit of bringing sales and marketing together is that it provides a great chance to increase effectiveness and of course focus. This is clearly seen in the lack of alignment of business structures when sales teams often organized regionally, by industry or by product. This is where the CSO has the chance to drive efficiency by making sure that all teams with the Smarketing department are aligned in the same way, at the very least to have micro teams that can deliver down the entire customer engagement funnel. Alignment is a key benefit of a single organizational approach with all teams, no matter the discipline, working closely together.

The objective for the CSO is to align execution down the engagement funnel

The objective of the CSO should be to create, align and integrate the sales and marketing teams to span the customer engagement cycle with consistent KPIs, reporting and incentivization. This will also allow the CSO to run a much more agile department, tapping into the other departments that support both sales and marketing in a much more efficient manner. We have touched on operations, but think of any department that supports these departments and engagement will be more effective with both aligned. Take the marketing manager, now part of integrated customer engagement for a specific industry or country, who now requests from their product marketing function some top-of-funnel assets to drive web traffic, and at the same time requests the content for every step down the engagement funnel and manages the passing of that content to the relevant people managing each step in the customer engagement process.

This is joined-up at inception and the thinking, design and execution will always benefit as a result. The CSO is the key to delivering the realized marketing department of the future and will be covered in more focus in the next chapter.

Smarketing is the merger of sales and marketing

Smarketing gets the best from all your resources

Smarketing is not just about sales and marketing alignment, it is also about being smart in the ways in which you engage with your customers. As we all know, resources and time are finite but many organizations act and work in a way that does not make the best use of either of these. It is never said in any company that sales and marketing have 'too much budget and too many staff' and therefore the aim of Smarketers and the CSO in particular is to drive the effectiveness of a company.

Schwerpunkt

As a business leader, a good place to look for examples of efficiency is the military, as throughout history human conflict has pushed us to the limits of thinking on effectiveness with the tools at hand. From Hannibal's attack on Rome with an inferior force from an unexpected direction, to combined arms tactics, war has always driven us to innovate in how to be more effective. One of the clearest examples of this that is highly relevant to Smarketers is the battle emphasis approach adopted by the Germans prior to World War II (WWII) that we may know more commonly as *blitzkrieg*. Simply put, this is a battle doctrine which advocates focusing resources on a single point or schwerpunkt in the line of engagement with an enemy to achieve a breakthrough that can then be exploited to achieve the wider objectives. When thinking of the use of resources in business, focusing is vital and bringing more resources to bear in a single area will drive incremental results. An old marketing adage to this point is to always run your sales promotion when you are running your advertising campaign, not sequentially. With a joined department the joining of activity becomes much simpler. There are a few specific areas where this efficiency is multiplied though, and these are worth highlighting further.

Account-based engagement

The first is in the area of account-based engagement for B2B companies, which is where a company focuses on a single specific target organization for its products or services. The aim of this is to convert that single organization into a customer and advocate. This approach is common in many businesses and even if there is not a formal programme it is still an approach used most widely within the sales organization. To deliver success this normally needs the focus of many departmental areas of a business coming together to drive the revenue from the specific selected target, but the reality is that the two departments that can have the biggest impact are sales and marketing. Within marketing there are often account-based marketing (ABM) programmes and experience within the teams linked to the focused selling approaches used by sales teams and it is this existing collaboration that benefits from a Smarketing organization. Once joined to this approach the engagement becomes easier to deliver and starts to drive the specificity of messaging and engagement that is a key outcome from Smarketing.

The terms MQL, BQL and SQL now need to be changed to MQA (marketing qualified account), BQA (business qualified account), and SQA (sales qualified account) to reflect the fact that we should be thinking about an account in the round, with multiple contacts, rather than an account in the singular as one person.

Joined-up sales and marketing messaging

Linking to this is the additional ability of a Smarketing organization to provide much more aligned messaging to its potential customers by the communication that is made possible by marketing and sales being organized together. With teams that are organized together the translation of industry or even organization challenges that can be addressed by the Smarketing business is much easier, with a flow of information from the sales teams at the virtual 'coal face' of customer engagement to the marketing teams more in the 'back office', where they can then take those messages and deliver them on scale back to the market to drive more engagement and, ultimately, business.

Rhiannon Prothero – Marketing Director UK & Ireland, SAP

If you're a small business with a dozen customers that's easy; if you're a big business with tens of thousands of customers it's not so easy, but my team works so closely with the individual sales teams we boil down the thousands of customers for each one of those to 15 or so. There is some review process that just happens on an ongoing basis because they are embedded as part of that sales team. How do we do that? Through old-fashioned human contact.

To illustrate this, imagine the sales rep in a meeting with a prospective client, who finds that his offering to the client exactly hits the spot for their current business needs and is seen as solving specific challenges for that business. The sales rep understands that this is not unique to the client they have just met but is also an issue for many other companies. On returning to the office the rep realizes that there are four other companies in their sales area that have this challenge and therefore starts to draft social media posts to engage those organizations.

It is at this point that they may be a good corporate citizen and pass this information wider via their management or network, but in many instances, realizing the overhead in time it would cost, this is not something that always happens or is even any form of objective for the rep. This is where, in a Smarketing organization, that sales rep would have direct engagement with marketing and in any regular feedback session marketing would be involved in capturing and understanding the opportunity as one that they can then take wider, building out a relevant marketing campaign. At every step this close alignment increases the efficiency of the company, its messaging and its progression of opportunity in the market.

In Smarketing organizations this direct connection then happens between sales and marketing. Thus it can feed directly into marketing content plans either for them to create one piece for everybody or to support the salesperson at the account level.

This view on efficiency is a key driver to the transformation to Smarketing and we believe is a key outcome of a successful integration of sales and marketing. As the technologies of sales and marketing evolve, a Smarketing organization will find the multiplication of efficiency increases and increases.

Digital buyer digital footprints – intent data

Each of your customers is leaving digital footprints when they search and review solutions; for example, asking questions on social, searching on Google, watching videos, looking at websites or reading content.

This intent information can be purchased on the open market and can be used in an integrated way across both marketing and sales, eg marketing-focused campaigns to reduce costs of advertising or social campaigns. Sales are able to use intent data so they can drill down into the topics they need to focus on in the next customer meeting. This is just one area where close alignment in the future could yield major benefits and allow the company adopting a Smarketing approach to blitz their way to success.

Customer journey challenge

When we look at the engagement process that all organizations have with their customers we see a clear journey that crosses both sales and marketing, yet separates at some point when customers are passed from marketing to sales. This separation in process, and potentially the resultant 'experience' for the customer, is one of the driving factors in customer dissatisfaction and a key reason why it must be addressed via a Smarketing transformation.

Depending on the products or services that an organization offers this 'hand-off' point will vary but it is there in all organizations and no matter the rigour applied to the process, making it invisible to the customer is often impossible. In some companies this is determined as the point when human interaction is introduced, with digital engagement the domain of marketing and the human process that of sales. In others, marketing will also include the initial qualification, possibly by chat or phone calls run by junior personnel. The issue with these approaches is that the journey that a customer experiences can be disjointed and this is often caused by the KPIs or targets of the respective divided departments.

In the modern business we need measures that the business can align and be measured against. These are called key performance indicators or KPIs for short. The challenge here is in aligning these KPIs to drive the right employee behaviour whilst also incentivizing and motivating without affecting the customer journey with your brand. Make the qualification too stringent and marketing may struggle to feed the sales requirement, too lax and sales may not value what they receive. This means that the major negotiation is at this point and in a well-structured organization it results in alignment of process, up to this point by marketing and from this point by sales.

Marketing build their processes to meet the qualification of MQL or MQA and sales then align to receive these and take them to their own SQL or SQA. Fundamentally this is where the concept of Smarketing has the most impact. Imagine defining the business clearly down the entire engagement process without a split between departments, no matter how small or smooth that may be. This is where a single management team led by a single CSO Smarketeer can remove this historical hand-off barrier. This also means that the responsibility for customer management is never handed off to a different part of the organization, thus maintaining the quality of interaction with the customer due to the allocation of responsibility within a single department. As outlined at the beginning of this chapter the ability of a business to survive today is determined by its ability to meet customer expectation, and providing a break in the customer experience hinders the business's ability to do that. This is compounded by the lack of visibility that a company has of why a customer may or may not pass to the next step in a process of engagement. With marketing reporting and managing up to the cut-off and sales beyond, the sharing of the details above and below that cut-off does not happen. This comes back to the earlier example of the car manufacturer and the fact that a change in web stats will indicate a change in sales figures.

With this visibility the sales team can plan and forecast better but in the Smarketing organization they can collaborate better to address the issue. This might result in the marketing team running social and advertising promotion based on intent data to a specific region around a dealership at the same time as sales organizing a promotion and test day with all the latest models, brought in from other dealerships and which might not normally be available.

Overall, the future Smarketing organization has just one key objective: to deliver a better customer experience and help the business respond better to customer needs. In all the businesses that we have reviewed and evaluated there is no better way to do this than by the joining of sales and marketing. When you think about the different parts of a business, the greatest volume of customer and prospect engagement comes from these two departments and the greatest value can be derived from them working together as a single entity.

Companies vary: sales-led – marketing-led – product-led

With the complexities of modern business, the way organizations work and the success that drives their working is hugely varied. However, the grouping of companies based on operational working and focus has always been the best way of classifying different company types and a Smarketing approach varies in its implementation and impact dependent on the company type. The standard classification used for many years is that there are broadly speaking three types of organization: sales led, marketing-led and product-led. For each of these we will touch on some of the differences in how Smarketing should be manifested and some of the areas of focus for each organization type.

So what are the differences between each?

- **Marketing-led company**: an organization which aims to determine what solutions or products a customer might want, and then guides the organization to develop those solutions or products. Such an organization relies heavily on market research and customer feedback.

- **Sales-led company**: an organization that focuses on sales teams driving throughput of its products and services within a defined, often short-term timeframe. These organizations need physical sales teams, either direct or indirect, to scale or provide increased revenue returns.

- **Product-led company**: an organization that focuses on developing product first, then establishing or finding a market for it. These organizations operate on the basis that with great products come customers which, in turn, brings in the profit and revenue.

Sales-led organization

For a sales-led organization we have seen the biggest challenge during the transformation to Smarketing is with the senior management, where sales leadership historically might have undervalued the contribution of marketing. This can make them resistant to the change to Smarketing and not buy into the process as it can often be seen as a reduction in their importance in the organization. It is for this reason that in sales-led organizations there is the need to drive this change from the CEO and normally to appoint an external person to the role of CSO.

Marketing-led organization

For a marketing-led organization we see that the empowerment and the promotion of the sales organization in importance has a significant effect on the quality of the customer experience. As the sales team feel they are a more integral part of the process of engaging customers rather than maybe just taking orders, the knock-on effect for the customer experience is positive. This allows the organization to get more feedback from their customers, which is the key lifeblood of these organizations. With an approach led by market information, getting more improved information can become a key differentiator in the market.

Product-led organization

We believe that in the future a new style of organization will appear – the Smarketing-led organization – as the unified role of CSO gains importance on the board. Their ability to provide a level of information that completes the picture the CFO provides will drive this change, just as the insight of this role and its combined operating units then starts to drive the direction of the organization for the ever more successful engagement of its customers.

Final thoughts on the CSO role

In the future the company with joined marketing and sales departments will be optimized in its given market. With visibility across its entire customer engagement cycle, a leader on the board of the importance of the CSO will have reporting responsibility on the entire process of interaction with customers and prospects. As well as providing feedback holistically, this allows the organization to engage more effectively and will be a vast improvement over a traditional approach to sales and marketing. Today all types of organizations operate in a competitive landscape, even if they have a monopoly where the competitors are cost and complacency, and as such all organizations need to optimize for the future. This brings us back to the introduction to this chapter and the numerous companies and organizations that have failed, and our view that Smarketing is a key approach to mitigating this risk.

Someone recently challenged us on this and suggested that this approach did not and should not apply to government organizations, which did spark a debate, but even for the public sector the requirement to engage their customer across every step in the process of interaction in a holistic way is vital. In the UK, British Rail (government-run train company) will always be remembered as an organization that fundamentally failed to understand its customer needs at a time when transport was changing massively. With a huge cost base and a lack of appreciation of the impact of the explosion in car sales and the development of motorways the organization did not anticipate its reduction in revenues from passengers.

Many years of price increases and cash injections from UK taxpayers did not change the direction of travel and eventually, after many years of being propped up by the government the business failed and was privatized, with the closure of many lines and massive changes in the offering of the railways. So how, one asks, would sales and marketing working together have helped this situation?

In those times it may have been unavoidable with a true visionary leading the organization, but today the signs would be there from the company's own data. With the third-party data available today they would be able to see and understand so much more. They would see a drop-off in advertising click-throughs, reduction in web traffic, shorter queues at ticket offices, less rubbish collected from the trains after use, and many more indicators, some longer-term projectors others more immediate. With a single internal organization seeing these things and understanding them, the ability to recognize the signs of concerns is massively increased. Without Smarketing, which organizations will succeed? With it, which organization will increase their chances of survival? In the following chapters we detail how you can make this move, with a detailed guide to delivering the Smarketing department of the future.

Conclusion

Siebel Systems, the market-leading CRM provider, before it was purchased by Oracle Corporation had under its logo the words, 'It is all about the customer'. Never has it been truer, and that customer is in control. We need to change our organizations to meet this new expectation in customer experience. No longer can we expect to offer the buyer a disjointed buying process, and we have talked about how the new role of CSO will enable management of that experience throughout the buying process, from the top of the funnel right through to close. This requires a new organization and a new language for these times of the internet and social media. No sales or marketing manager has ever said, 'we have enough resources', yet by merging sales and marketing we can achieve great efficiencies and effectiveness. In effect, more revenue for less investment by the business.

Questions to ask yourself

1 Does your sales and marketing team have a common language; will sales agree with marketing as to what is defined as a lead?

2 Are you a product-, sales- or marketing-led organization? Is that right for where your business is right now in terms of development? If it is not, how could you change it?

3 In terms of your own Smarketing programme, will you aim for one leader or maintain a culture of cooperation but keep two leaders?

4 Following up from the question in the last few chapters, on the basis that no sales or marketing department has infinite resources, do you think a 'schwerpunkt' programme might help you channel resources?

5 Without stalking, are you collecting and measuring the digital footprints of your prospects and customers in terms of things like intent data?

Reference

Brady, C and Mullins, J W (2005) *End of the Road: True story of the downfall if Rover*, Prentice Hall, Harlow

Preparing for Smarketing in your company

05

When it comes down to it, nothing trumps execution.
GARY VAYNERCHUCK

So how do we move to the future state of sales and marketing that we have outlined in the previous chapter? Making this change is not insignificant for a business and represents change across a number of dimensions and business units within the organization. Often delivering change in a way that not only achieves the outcome but also does not compromise the day-to-day output of the organization is difficult. As such, having a clear approach and path to achieve Smarketing is vital if you and your business are to have any chance of success in your Smarketing transformation. With any transformation, there are a lot of varied factors that can not only affect any change but also slow or compromise it, so a structured approach is vital.

When looking at the best approach to driving this transformation we believe that focusing on four key pillars of change is fundamental. These pillars are strategy, people, process and stakeholders. With focus on the plan for each of these pillars you can make the transition to Smarketing and deliver the transformed organization including the optimizations that will follow for your organization, as outlined later in Chapter 8.

The first pillar – strategy

As with any major business project a clear approach is needed to make sure that the end game is achieved. In Chapter 6 we will explore

Figure 5.1   The pillars of Smarketing

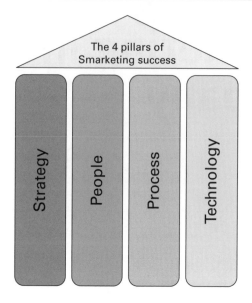

this to provide the clear steps on how to drive the transformation to Smarketing, but this chapter shows the outline of how to establish the main high-level steps to Smarketing.

Strategy leadership

For any major strategy, a business needs to nominate a leader to be the figurehead but also to be accountable and to drive the breadth of the organization towards the goal. In the transformation to Smarketing this is no different and the Smarketing leader that we outlined in the previous chapter is the person that needs to lead this change. As detailed, with their skills across marketing and sales they need to always be the unifying visionary to drive this change. If you think about even the smallest project, one clear leader that has a view of all the different actions for the project is vital, and the Smarketing leader needs to be that person.

From a day-to-day point of view, it often works well to have a tactical supporter of the leader to make sure that the actions are captured and processed. So, to achieve success the Smarketing leader needs to make this their first appointment to the transformation team. The type of individual that is well suited to this role is a marketing or sales operations senior executive with good project and change management experience. Often a person that is relatively new to the organization will be best suited, as they are not too burdened by the legacy of their time in the company. They will be able to support the Smarketing leader throughout the process of transforming to Smarketing and help to drive the organization to achieve each step-by-step objective in the transformation project as a whole.

A key part of their role will be to manage a single view of the project and the sub-objectives that make up each stage, as well as running the regular update meetings to maintain this view and receive a clear update from the different business leaders that make up the transformation team. We will come to this in the following chapter, as well as what that transformation team should look like.

Maintaining the dialogue

With a leader in place, the first thing that needs to be determined is the communication approach that will help to keep all parties within the organization up to date on the transformation project. As we all know, communication is pivotal to maintaining buy-in and support within any group of people; a lack of communication is a huge threat to a change process of this scale. Measured against this are the risks of over-communication and inappropriate information being passed out that might cause issues either internally or externally, as change can often be negatively perceived. For this reason, a structured communications approach needs to be adopted and setting this is one of the first key tasks. A straightforward approach to communications is needed to set three levels of information that will be passed out: company-wide communication, Smarketing team management communication, and tactical change team communication.

The first is the high-level communication that should be sent to the whole organization in the name of the Smarketing leader, with the endorsement and support of the senior management. This should take the form of a monthly or quarterly newsletter on the transformation to Smarketing, with key high-level information about why the project has been undertaken, the key team members and the main milestones in the transformation. It is important that this does not include too much detail but conveys the drive of the business and the important pieces of information that help to get all staff on the same page in understanding the process and outcomes that Smarketing is looking to – and will – achieve.

Internal communication at this level can often be lost within the noise of the day job so this is not just about sending an e-mail to staff; there needs to be face-to-face communication and a persistent location where this update lives, such as the intranet. As with any major business change, running all-hands meetings followed by regular departmental updates with open Q&A sessions will enable all members of the business to stay updated, engaged and, most importantly, bought into the project. An additional outcome of this is often that outspoken staff can be brought into the process by giving them roles or tasks as part of the transformation that fit their skills, thus helping turn any detractors into advocates or advocates into champions.

Management communication needs to complement this organizational communication and maintain a level of regularity that helps to keep management buy-in. Taking similar approaches to those used at the company level but running them to the management team will help to drive the process of change from the top down. There are two main types of management communication; the first is to the Smarketing transformation management team and needs to include a regular face-to-face meeting where each key leader of elements of the project brings their update, which is documented by the Smarketing leader and the tactical project management supporter.

The publishing of the project summary to this group, with a simple traffic light dashboard, will then allow them to understand where the project is and see clearly the steps to come and who owns them. Depending on the scale of the organization this can be a challenging group to bring together, but it is vital, and the larger the business the more focus needs to be placed on the importance of attendance at these updates either in person or via video conferencing. One approach that can help in this process is the appointment of deputies for the main members of the Smarketing management team.

The other types of communication relate to the actions that make up the project plan and each of the owners of these tasks that form the transformation team are responsible, with their deputies, for delivering the communication.

Metrics, measurement and accountability

At an early stage of the process, and as a key part of the strategy, metrics need to be set for the change to succeed. This is an opportunity to look again at the metrics for the whole organization across the whole customer engagement cycle. We will look in more detail at this in Chapter 8 but here we outline the drivers behind measurement selection and the various levers one should consider that fit and work to support and facilitate the strategy.

The core business metrics are the main area of substantial change that need to be re-worked and decisions need to be made about how far this goes, and therefore how much of a re-work is applied. The aim here, which should never be forgotten, is to improve the interaction with customers whilst enabling staff to deliver at each part of this interaction. This is the core need for change and in many businesses this is the biggest issue, where siloed departments have their own metrics that are not part of the wider customer interaction. Some simple examples of this, as touched on earlier in the book, are where you might have a last touch attribution model in marketing or a sales opportunity conversion target for telesales reps. As such, this needs to change and focus must move to a more integrated approach.

We have shown the engagement funnel previously and it is when using this that an organization needs to look at its technology and the ways that it might implement sensible metrics alongside that engagement funnel. We will cover this more fully in Chapter 8, but one example of this would be measurement approaches from account-based marketing, and this may form the core for the metrics change. In many organizations, interest in new offers or products is often measured as some form of lead; this is then tracked across the various departments from marketing lead to tele-lead to sales, to potential close and revenue in the bank.

Figure 5.2   Changing the nature of measurement

Traditional measurement

Responses, Leads, Opportunities, Revenue

Smarketing measurement

Intent, Account Engagement, Customer Satisfaction

We chose this example as this is exactly the interaction that we need to move away from in many B2B organizations. Moving to a state where every interaction is measured allows you to look at things on a company or account basis. This is where, in account-based approaches to customer engagement, you would look at an Account Engagement Score or Account Conversion Rating. This score, as detailed in Chapter 8, is the sum of all the interactions with an account, sitting above the individual elements like leads that make up the interaction with that organization. It might seem a simple change but the aim here is to align the metrics to a joined-up approach for customer engagement.

Evolving staff skills

Another element of the measurement to achieve Smarketing is a clear and measurable plan to move over the current workforce to the new approach, and a vital part of this is the training that they will need. Ultimately the approach here will come down to other decisions about moving to Smarketing and the current skills, outlook and aspirations of the workforce in sales and marketing. As such we cannot list the training that is required but there are some key principals to the agenda which will allow this part of the process to be successful.

First, an attitude of 'can do' passed down across the whole department from the new Smarketing leader. This needs to be passed on by every line manager to their staff as it's only through the individual members of the teams that true transformation to Smarketing will be delivered. Every member of staff needs to feel that they are part of the journey and that they can contribute and provide input rather than solely having a new approach dictated to them. Often during change projects, in order to facilitate this ethos becoming reality there needs to be specific training of the first-line management in the organization. This can be undertaken as a top-down briefing from the Smarketing leader for the key elements of the project and a viewpoint on how the management should conduct them, and then some HR-led training, possibly from external experts, on how managers can deliver change projects. We have touched on some of the human challenges previously and similarly this applies here for the first-line management of an organization and their ability to lead, manage expectations, address dissenters and build a positive, evolved view of all the staff.

Second, a necessary element is detailed skills training, which we touch on later in this chapter, to give all the relevant roles the ability to understand better the roles that sit before and after them in the customer engagement cycle. An example of this would be for the marketing experts to gain more sales process training to understand the steps the customers will go through beyond the marketing they used to previously focus on.

Reorganizing the business

When looking at the measurement of the organization there has to be a clear plan to reorganize and metrics to achieve that reorganization. The Smarketing leadership need to define the terms of the reorganization and then work with their senior management to drive through a timeline to achieve the reorganization (re-org). The start of this is to outline what a target operating model for Smarketing could look like based on the business and its subsequent objectives. This target operating model should include a core summary of the main areas of reorganization within sales and marketing as well as an outline of the structure post-reorganization. Aligned to timelines and empowerment this will allow the management team to measure and adjust as the organization changes.

The challenge pillar – people

The hardest part of changing the organization to Smarketing is in evolving the roles and responsibilities of the staff. As outlined, this is why it's key to have a strong leader, and now we cover the approaches that can be taken in order to help facilitate this change. As every organization is different, we will suggest examples that might apply to your industry but there are too many different types of organization and industry to list all the organizational structures that would work. As such we will focus below on the approaches and steps that will help to make this step successful.

How to organize people

In bringing these two departments together, the main elements of the reorganization are about aligning common roles, so this should be the core of the structure of the Smarketing department. Aligning operations, HR and supporting functions immediately is key. Referring to measurement, for example, only an integrated operations team would be able to do this along the whole customer engagement cycle and move to some key metric such as the account engagement score that would give a single measurable view of the client's organization. For HR, being able to align recruitment of sales and marketing individuals also has huge benefits; applying the same core principals to recruitment allows alignment before staff even join the company. A basic example of this is that the brief for recruitment has similar high-level elements such as industry background, university degree (or not), and competitor knowledge.

It is when an organization gets to its actual front-line sales, marketing and management that more options for uniquely setting the structure come about. It is here that the majority of the work needs to focus on getting things right to give the right customer experience. We look in more detail in the next chapter at some of the ways to establish or set the restructure.

When it comes to the actual implementation of the reorganization there are a number of ways that this can be undertaken. This will depend very much on a number of factors:

- the size of the organization and the extent of the proposed change;
- the time period in which the board wants to see this done;
- the propensity for external review and guidance.

And then the approach that management decide based on these factors will take a number of different forms:

- **Mandated**: Senior management drive the move to the new organization centrally, with limited flexibility during the process for changing decisions. This allows for much faster change but often misses certain key customer engagement challenges or opportunities and can result in staff alienation and failing to achieve the actual objective of improved customer interaction.

- **Managed**: Senior management empower mid management to drive the transformation with more feedback, possibility for adapting processes and changing structural decisions. This may be seen as the right balance, allowing for a degree of pace whilst at the same time getting the right outcome for customers and staff.

- **Consulted**: Senior management look for suggested options from the mid-level and first-line management of how their respective departments might look post-transformation, allowing for many more options being fielded but a lot more flexibility in the establishment of the final structure. This might provide the best ultimate structure but may also be far too time-consuming to deliver effectively, although if the right process is applied this may be the best approach to take.

Whatever approach is taken it is key to support the staff in this process and to make sure that the culture of the change is supportive. As mentioned, the management, particularly the first-line management, need to be trained and empowered, as this is key to success: we cannot highlight this enough. If this training and support is delivered effectively there are many benefits. One example might be in empowering negativity and taking detractors through steps to make them valued supporters of the transformation. This often only takes straightforward management techniques of listening, documenting and feeding back on the outcomes of any objection to help the person feel heard and that their criticisms are then becoming part of the thinking driving the transformation.

How to enable staff

We have touched on how key it is to identify training for staff at every level of seniority through this process of change, to mitigate the human issues that inevitably arise in any change project. Bear in mind that any re-enablement of staff can be used to standardize views or skills and not just applied to staff without a particular skill or experience. Here we summarize the main types of training that need to be factored into the process and should be delivered across the organization:

- **External training**: Working with key third parties that have relevant training courses will be vital to success. This will be a case of selecting the right organizations to be able to train staff in the areas where they need more enablement.

- **Internal training**: Leveraging internal experts able to transfer skills and knowledge to build new courses tailored specifically to your organization for particular skills or knowledge.

- **Advocate training**: Similar to above but these staff may not be historical trainers, rather experts at what they do who can take a subject and pass it on, often more informally. This can also be a way to empower staff and get their buy-in to transformation by making them virtual leaders for specific subjects and areas.

- **Management training**: Using the management of the organization to train teams can be a very effective way to quickly and cheaply re-enable the organization whilst aligning to the culture of the organization. Management often have the requisite skills to do this, as well as knowledge of the existing approaches and process, to allow for a clear articulation of any areas that are changing.

Overall, when it comes to the training of the organization it's key to move fast and learn fast from the feedback received by the trainers in areas that might be contentious. Training feedback should be a key tool of the management team in gauging the staff's ability, drive and propensity to move to Smarketing.

The final point to cover from a personnel point of view is the selection of new staff to expand or replace the existing talent. For any department going through a major change it's important to secure the right people to be able to support that project and then thrive afterwards. When looking for the right Smarketing individuals there are three main things to look for:

- First, experience across multiple disciplines, whether within sales or marketing or actually across the two. We often see staff moving from one to the other in their careers and these are key individuals to target due to their cross-Smarketing experience.

- Second, successful experience in multiple companies showing an ability to adapt well, as there will be constant change in moving to Smarketing. As you may adjust the department in various ways you need a team that can deal with this and respond positively during these periods.

- Third, passion and motivation, often the hardest things to ascertain but a vital part of the make-up of these new Smarketeers. The desire to challenge and innovate will help set the basis for your Smarketing success as the department grows and evolves.

The velocity pillar – process

For any modern organization the processes of the company are vital to its operations. Normally evolved either over many years of internal experience or from external best practice, they are the bedrock of the business and shape the customer interaction. Due to the complexity that relates to process and the way that it is hard-coded into the business from staff to systems to documentation to culture, this is the biggest challenge when evolving to Smarketing. However, it is one of the key pillars to address and evolve, and with a clear framework this can be done effectively. Even taking a potential challenge area like IT, for example the Customer Relationship Management (CRM) and Enterprise Resource Planning (ERP) systems that support sales and marketing, with a process to incremental change this can still be evolved.

Approaches to evolved process – journey mapping

Taking the challenges outlined above it is important that any change to processes is done in a way that actually achieves the outcome that is needed for the customer and the business. For this reason, and to achieve such a large change as the transformation to Smarketing, we believe that using journey mapping is the safest approach. Borne out of customer experience (CX) consulting approaches as a way for businesses to understand the multiple dimensions of engagement with their customers, it's a great way to determine the key process changes to make.

At its core, journey mapping should look at the steps along the customer engagement cycle taken by the Smarketing department, the systems aligned to these departments, and the customer. Looking at the journeys next to each other allows us to see the current state, optimal state and the changes needed to reach the optimal state. Since its inception as a service design approach in 1999 for a high-speed rail project, it has been taken and adopted by many businesses.

A great example was when a major industrial manufacturer used this approach to increase the use of computerized tomography (CAT) scanners for children. The issue they had was that hospitals reported very low usage rate of their scanners for children and the engineers were surprised by this as the technology was first rate. It turned out, after mapping the child's journey through the use of a CAT scanner, that it was a very intimidating process and from the first meeting with the doctor was positioned badly, meaning the children did not actually want to enter the scanner.

A few changes later and the whole journey was changed for the child. A story was applied to the machine, for example the child was going on a ship, entering the jungle or exploring a secret cave. No longer is the machine standard white but is now painted with graphics to be part of the story, with lots for the child to look at and always the offer that their favourite teddy can go first. For the purpose of Smarketing it is vital to use this approach to maintain alignment to the customer engagement cycle and to make sure that the hidden divides in customer engagement are uncovered, such as with this example.

We will detail this more fully in the next chapter and talk about how the organization can work together to make sure the journey evolves to provide the right outcomes without too much change to the expensive or less flexible aspects such as technology.

Implementing process transformation

Once the core process approaches are determined and established via journey mapping it is then necessary to evaluate whether these can be implemented in the organization and how easy it will be to do so. There are many views on applying process change and transformation which we will not go into here in detail, but we will summarize some of the key points to give you a framework to use for your decision making in how to implement the transformation from your journey mapping.

Completion of journey mapping

Document the entire outcome from the journey mapping and outline the main changes that need to be made as a result. Clear documentation needs to be started at this point, with ownership applied to the steps of change detailed from the journey mapping

Outline process change plan

A plan then needs to build up, detailing and documenting the changes and owners followed by the timeframes of change for each step. Additionally, you can set key objectives in and around each area of change identified by the journey mapping to help the teams focus. The ownership of each process change needs to have a full team of appropriately skilled individuals who are capable of delivering the process in its new form.

Detailing the processes

The team can then work on detailing the minutiae of the process and the changes for the area that they are responsible for. A vital part of this step is to make sure that various options are offered so that an optimal approach can be selected based on testing and outcome

Figure 5.3   Define your process change teams

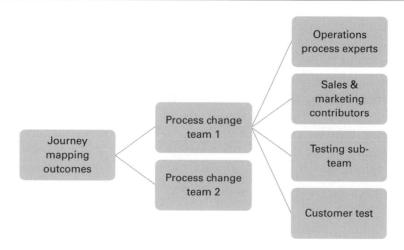

rather than gut feel. Even though we have talked about being joined-up, due to the size of this task it is rarely possible for a single team to deliver it. As shown in Figure 5.3, having a clear process change team with a structure to feed into a single view aligned to the outcomes of the journey mapping is key.

With a clear team and structure for managing any changes, any process change that is suggested by the journey mapping can be passed to a team for delivery. Each team has to have the right individuals to detail and then execute the process change with the appropriate testing and customer validation. Any process change must be tested with customers to confirm the impact and make sure that there is improvement over the previous approach.

Stress testing

Once a process is detailed it can then be tested prior to being taken live. A key step in the overall change delivery is at this point when the team can also evaluate alternatives. Taking two or three options for a step or series of steps and checking which works best is vital to ultimately delivering the best customer experience. Some of the testing here might be live in the business and may involve agile pilot projects that build up the understanding of what might work. It should also be noted that it can often be an area of great engagement for staff to run these often exciting and important projects helping to enthuse and empower team members. It does require vision and leadership in the delivery of any pilots and tests to make sure that they are done well; don't get bogged down in internal blocks, either people or technology, that might hinder them.

Launch of process

Once the options for the changes have been tested the results can be passed up the process team to determine the actual changes for moving to an initial new state of the Smarketing process. This should be combined with internal communication from the Smarketing leader and training as required to get all relevant staff bought in prior to the launch.

Continual improvement

After a major change to processes there will be additional updates needed on an ongoing basis to refine things and optimize them. This should be a cyclical part of the steps that is done regularly to allow for continual improvement.

Beyond the steps for delivering the process change to Smarketing it is key to include the other parts of the business. There are many supporting parts of the business that need to be involved and having an approach for this is vital. Other departments like HR, finance, product engineering, development, consulting, etc, all need to be part of this transformation and the process change as they will all be impacted by it one way or another. One way to drive this is to have individuals from these departments aligned to the overall project. This can be simply achieved by placing them into the project teams looking at delivering the outcomes of the journey mapping. Or it may be that there is a separate virtual team set up with these nominated individuals and some of the management from the Smarketing team. Either way, regular updates should be driven out across the organization. A point to note on embedding staff from other departments in the process change teams is that they can make sure that their departments' processes are factored in. A danger is that they can slow things down, but overall inclusion is important with change on this scale.

When looking at which teams to include it is important for the Smarketing leader to make suggestions to the board of who to include and to make sure that they are bought in to supporting. When looking at which other departments to include, bear in mind the ones most affected by the change and the ones that can help the most to make it successful. If departments are not included they may not be bought in to the outcome of the change or may be disruptive after Smarketing is implemented, looking back to the pre-state as superior. Avoiding any of these issues is vital and a key focus of the Smarketing leadership. It is worth reiterating here the importance of the board/ C-suite and senior leadership in delivering this transformation. This cannot be underestimated, as without the direct support of the likes of the CEO and CFO, such buy-in will be hard to secure from other parts of the business.

The final point to factor in for delivering the process change is the importance of sales and marketing operations. Ultimately it's the operations functions in a business that maintain and run the process, the system and the people, so they need to be the owners of this part of the change. We have already touched on securing a single operations lead as the support to the Smarketing leader; this role is key and should be the first change you make. That person then leading this transformation and sitting at the top of the process change team's hierarchy will help to give a consistent vision and drive to the change delivery. Operations become the guardians of the momentum of transformation to Smarketing, as they should be.

The recognition pillar – stakeholders

Coming to the final pillar for the transformation we will focus on the other stakeholders that are affected by the change to Smarketing. We have touched on a few points relating to this in the previous paragraphs, but now we bring together the key points to factor in to drive the successful implementation of Smarketing.

So, having decided to go down the route to Smarketing it is vital to start and maintain regular communication to all other departments and the board. We will start with communicating to the other departments.

Whatever the size of the organization people will respond best to personal communications from people that they know and respect, and it is with this in mind that the structure of the internal communications should be established. In order for an effective plan of communications to be built and delivered it is also vital for it to have a clear owner, and someone trusted by the Smarketing leader should be selected. As this is often already part of marketing it makes sense for the person to be from that department, with a background in communications that they can leverage to build and drive the execution of the wider communications plan to the rest of the business. Simple techniques such as regular videos updating on specific areas of change from the department leaders can be very effective and simple to do using a smart phone with suitable video recording capability. If this is not the sort of communication that is appropriate for your organization, then clear written information alongside face-to-face updates will also work. For example, as an industry team of marketers and sales representatives combines, that team leader joins the HR team's regular meeting to brief on the status, what's different, and the impact on any HR support that the industry team might get.

With a person in place and an outline to the approach, a detailed plan should be delivered that the Smarketing leader can view and see if it is being completed. A matrixed approach can work here to see clearly that 'Team A' has been updated on 'Change B'. The level to which this is done depends on the size of the organization but overall clear tracking is necessary, as without visibility it's impossible to understand how well the organization is being taken through the steps of change.

Smarketing results

In order for the senior stakeholders to buy in to the implementation of Smarketing it is clearly the results that are the most important thing and as such should be the core of all reporting up. This is where the Smarketing leader will be focusing a lot of their time in the initial stages of the transformation to Smarketing, working to make sure that the board are bought in and respond well to the changes that are happening.

There are some key points to establishing the board buy-in and the leader needs to address these with each member. At this high level we wanted to highlight the main three points to be aware of, although you can of course break this down more:

- The first point is to communicate to each person individually and reference their department or area of control so that they clearly understand what the outcome will be for them. This will help them to understand the benefits for them and why they should care in the first place.

- The second point is to share on a regular basis the overall plan, from its inception with the initial business case to the updates at regular board meetings with short, concise progress summaries and outcomes to date. This is about transparency and should also include specific focus on the different members of the board and numbers or outcomes that relate to each.

- The final point is more fundamental and is about how they perceive their viewpoints are being considered. It is important that all board members (and even any senior stakeholders) feel they are being taken seriously and that their ideas, objections and thoughts are taken seriously. With a major change project like this it's far too easy for executives to get sidelined and drop their support.

The language of change

The final point to make about communication from the Smarketing department across all stakeholders is the need for consistent language and terminology. This is vital so that at all levels people are saying the same things and communicating consistently. This might seem obvious but it's too easy to allow a bottom-up approach to terminology so this needs to be rationalized and managed before being passed out to the wider teams. In large organizations it often happens that there are two or three different names for the same thing, especially where cross-departmental projects are concerned. With a single internal communications leader supporting the Smarketing leader this becomes much more avoidable. The aim here is a centrally defined glossary of internal terms that is short, clear and concise to help drive efficiency, clarity and avoid confusion. This approach should also be applied to any numbers that are shared as part of the project; they must also be consistent across the communications.

Conclusion

Without a clear approach to delivering such major change, a business will not be able to find a way to move to Smarketing. It is key that there is a clearly laid out path for the business that all the staff within the company can follow. An understanding of the major steps in preparing for Smarketing and the key factors to be evaluated will help to achieve an effective outcome and our aim here has been to lay the essentials out. The key conclusion we want to pass on is the importance of these but also the importance of the people with and around these steps. For those who have been through change projects in the past you will know that it's the people who make them happen and this is no different. All of the pillars we have outlined above revolve around people and with them in place the business can then move to the actual plan for delivering Smarketing and the steps that entails.

Questions to ask yourself

1 Who are your key stakeholders that you need to influence as part of your Smarketing programme? In what ways will you approach them differently?

2 Assuming you are willing to burn political capital to implement a Smarketing programme, do you understand your stakeholders' personal wins? Do you understand the blockers?

3 How will you get the stakeholders' buy-in now and continued buy-in as you work through the project?

4 Can you see 'quick wins' that you can work on and communicate out to the wide team and audience?

5 Do you have a customer journey map that all can see? Is this an ongoing developing thing?

How do you implement a Smarketing transformation?

06

Strategy is the starting point for a transformation that needs to occur and how that company must change to win.
LYNNE DOUGHTIE

Introduction

Now that we have set the scene for the evolution to Smarketing and laid the key precepts that you need to set up we will take you through the process for moving to Smarketing. When looking to this we have taken the approach to outline a series of clear steps to follow, and this eight-step methodology is detailed in this chapter.

The implementation

Overall, this journey should be taken in clear incremental steps to allow the organization to adjust without compromising the business. It is critical to avoid rushing change programmes that might cause issue to profitability or the day-to-day running of the organization.

As such, these steps aim to start the process by taking what you already have in the organization and evolving it to Smarketing with small incremental changes step by step. When undertaking this phased approach always think of each step in the context of your business and the benefit that can be gained; think of the law of increasing returns

Figure 6.1   Focus on the areas that make the biggest impact

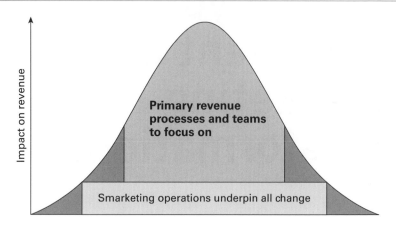

when reviewing the steps to make sure that a large effort is not applied in an area which has limited impact and effect on the overall customer engagement cycle. Another approach is to use a bell curve evaluation approach to determine the areas that have the most impact on the business and focus on those first.

Step 1 – Gather the team

The first step is to gather the core team around the Smarketing leader. These individuals need to be selected from existing marketing and sales management based on their skills, experience and their role within the existing organization. As we have outlined already, the first team that needs to be aligned to Smarketing is the operations organization, combining sales and marketing operations. In Chapter 8 we will cover the core activities of this team in more detail but to provide project management, reporting, metric and governance management it is vital to have the Smarketing operations team in place. There are many different approaches after this first step for how to set up the organization, which will be based upon your business objectives and the regional, product or specialism-based requirements that the business might have. It will also vary depending on the type of organization; as outlined in Chapter 4, sales-led, marketing-led or product-led originations will all need a slightly different approach to the set-up. Below we summarize the core components that should be considered after the operations team is in place.

Core Smarketing teams

The following bullet points outline the teams that need to be part of the Smarketing organization and the tasks, attributes and abilities of these teams. We have also given a guide here as to the weighting towards marketing or sales skills that over time will blend, but this should help to understand the outlook of these teams.

- **Operations team**: The support team for sales and marketing that provides systems, processes and analytics support. A vital team that underpins all that Smarketing does.

- **Field teams**: The execution teams that deliver the actual sales and marketing into markets that are being targeted. Marketing focuses on the early stages of customer engagement and sales manages the completion of a transaction.

- **Web team**: Building, delivering and managing the web real estate of the organization.

- **Project teams**: Groups drawn together from across the department to deliver specific projects. These are often temporary teams but in large organizations may include a team that moves from project to project as needed.

- **Management team**: The senior leadership of the Smarketing department that manages each area including any regional or product-related groups.

- **Content team**: A focused team to deliver the information in any format for both internal and external uses to support communication. This could be customer-facing messaging or enablement information for internal teams; the ideal is a single team linking the two types of information.

- **Training team**: Part of the department specifically focused on internal enablement of the various teams across the Smarketing department.

Working practice

Irrespective of the set-up of the organization there needs to be a great focus on the working practice that the joined department adopts in the way it works. It is very important that the leadership are able to instil in the teams a core of adaptability, flexibility, innovation and collaboration. This should be done through a number of mechanisms that the management teams should be comfortable to implement and be supported with training if they are not. The key ways this can be done are:

- **Examples set by the leadership**: Having senior management engage directly with more junior team members, regular all-hands meetings, promotion of new ideas shown to be adopted by management. Overall this will be a key part of their leadership and if enablement is required to allow the manager to work in this way it should be prioritized.

- **Use of cross-departmental teams**: Taking members from varied teams to form key working groups; it might be they are running a pilot to test, or looking at an operational part of the business via SWOT (Strengths, Weakness, Opportunities and Threats) analysis. Bringing different teams together in small groups is a great way to build a strong, knowledgeable and skilled Smarketing department.

- **Ideas promotions**: Offering all staff the ability to volunteer ideas for improvements, promotions or any aspect of sales and marketing. This can be operational, customer orientation or any dimension of the department and could be anonymous or not, depending on the type of ideas approach. One way is to brand it and give it a simple identifier that everyone can clearly understand, like 'Ideas Factory'.

The final part of the working methodology should be the adoption of some of the principles of Agile in the working approach. Agile approaches to task completion date back to the late 1990s and software development, with many books written on the subject, but for the purposes of sales and marketing and in particular the type of business transformation we outline here, it is ultimately a process to work fast and understand outcomes fast. In effect, work fast, win or fail fast, the approach being to then move quickly to the next iteration and overall achieve the objective quicker than might normally be expected. Below are outlined the key steps of what we see as an Agile approach for Smarketing:

1 Establish and agree objective to be delivered.

2 Confirm the team to deliver on the objective including a leader, roles and responsibilities.

3 Set cadence of short daily updates for the project team, preferably face to face for 30 minutes.

4 Agree the main steps to deliver the project and break this down across the team.

5 Focus the team with clear daily tasks driven by daily updates.

6 The leader must challenge the outcomes of the team to stress test that the individual outcomes are moving towards the objective.

7 Bring the whole team together to reflect to become more effective and adjust based on the feedback.

A final point to make is when drawing together a team and instilling a specific working practice, this team should develop a positive character of its own that will develop over time. The best traits of character can be summarized with words like trustworthy, dependable, efficient, responsible and these are the sorts of things for the leadership to promote within their team. To achieve this will take time, work, a clear sense of teamwork and a lot of support from management, but is vital for long-term success. A sanity check of this could for example be for a colleague from another part of the business to question a team member about the benefits of the Smarketing programme; could they clearly and quickly articulate the benefits and the direction of travel for the programme?

Step 2 – Understand the organization

The next key step is the detailed mapping and categorization of the main dimensions of the business. This will allow you and the operations department to map out and plan changes and alterations appropriately.

Sales and marketing

Detail the full sales and marketing organization, taking note to outline the size, focus, results and responsibilities of each area.

Highlight the departments that can be aligned as a Smarketing team, such as field marketing and sales.

Separate the main function within each that might not be so straightforward to merge, such as public relations (PR), event support, web team, CRM support, sales support, pre-sales, or technical sales.

Determine if there are individuals within the team who could align to Smarketing teams. For example, the web team might be able to provide resource to cover the main industry pages or regional pages, therefore becoming virtual members of that Smarketing field team; the same might apply for all supporting functions.

Other departments

Summarize the other key departments that the Smarketing organization will have to integrate with and outline the impact on each, if any. As the actual day-to-day function of selling and marketing does not fundamentally change, the impact should be limited, except for HR, where hiring support needs to evolve.

The main departments that must be factored in are Finance, Business Operations, Office of the Chief Executive, Training, Product development, Production (manufacturing) and HR.

Regions

How does this transformation work across regions and how should you organize as a result? All this needs to be considered and evaluated. This is a key role of the management team after taking feedback and input from planning teams and Smarketing operations.

The reality is that the more complex the current structure, the more the move to Smarketing will simplify it by consolidating teams and reducing lines of communication.

It is also key as part of this to provide a model and ethos within the teams that anticipates more change. Ultimately, the need is for a dynamic business that can constantly change rather than a structure set in stone for an extended period of time.

Customers

Summarize the different customer groups that the organization is engaging. As part of this exercise you should also re-run any market sizing and market potential analysis. This will allow for the effective redistribution of the resources as it is vital to use this transformation to align to the potential revenue opportunities in the market.

This is also the time to check and analyse the status of existing customers as the alignment of Smarketing for them can have the very positive impact of increasing customer satisfaction.

At the senior management level, the understanding of potential revenues is important and should be a key driver in the transformation. Most B2B businesses generate 90 per cent of their revenue from 10 per cent of their customers, so part of the aim of Smarketing alignment is to extend the profitability of more target customers to increase beyond the 10 per cent.

External impacts

The final groups to factor into this evaluation are the external organizations and resources that might support or be impacted by the process of moving to Smarketing or by the changed business at the other end.

For suppliers and other organizations that might be in the supply chain, openness and transparency will be pivotal to reducing any issues. It is here that through the management team a culture of transparency will have it first in passing this information outside the business.

For partners, whether they are small or large, a similar approach should be taken. Depending on where the partner management team sits within the organization this may be more straightforward or require specific focus and effort.

As the nature of the company's business is not changing, though, partners should see limited fundamental change but will maybe have different teams to liaise with or changed processes.

If the partner team is separate, specific communication should be undertaken to involve them, take input and provide constant updates on the move to Smarketing.

As outlined here, there are many teams that will be impacted by the move to Smarketing and getting a clear view of these and the impact is key. As an early step this will be one of the first projects that needs to be completed before the subsequent steps can be initiated. It will form a good first task for the joined Smarketing operations team to undertake, as the information that needs to be gathered and detailed comes historically from both sales and marketing.

A key part of the analysis that the Smarketing operations team can also review is the initial suggestions on ways to work smarter. This move to Smarketing has a few core objectives and smarter working is a key one of those we have touched on; this analysis is the initial manifestation of the direction this could take. This is more than just aligning marketing and sales – it's about getting smarter as well.

Step 3 – What to change

Now that we have the core information and initial outline of the parts of the business, including the effect on each, we can move to detail the actual changes to make to processes and departments. In this book we have detailed many suggestions for different dimensions of a business but cannot fundamentally provide an outline for all types of businesses in all industries. Therefore, as mentioned in the previous chapter, this step should include a customer journey mapping process that allows the right changes to be suggested.

The outcome of this journey mapping process should achieve the following:

- What is the outcome for the customer?
- Which are the key areas of the engagement to transform?
- What are the changes in our operating procedure that will affect the customer?

To assist in delivering a journey mapping process, here are the key steps to follow:

1 Identify team: Bring together a group of roughly 30 people from across the different customer touchpoints within the whole business. This team is the core that will run this process and gather input from the various parts of the organization.

2 **Interview business**: Run a questionnaire via the above team across their individual areas to provide a broader input. This questioning must be focused on ideas for improvement, both internal and external. For example, do not ask what is broken but what could make X process better for customers and, separately, for employees.

3 **Draft mapping**: With teamwork, go through the customer engagement cycle and map each touchpoint from a customer, systems, process and employee point of view.

4 **Review mapping**: Get the team together to walk through the journey and provide input from all teams. This is improved if there is a customer involved. It may be that multiple outcomes are derived from this step.

5 **Running the journey**: Take the outcomes from the review step and run tests within the business to determine true suitability.

6 **Core conclusions**: Take the most successful confirmed changes and select key individuals within the team to document these in detail. This must include the clear documented results that the changes have delivered.

7 **Deliver the findings**: Change the business with the findings of the journey mapping.

The outcome of this workshop should be to identify key areas for change that moving to Smarketing can drive to improve customer engagement. As touched on in the steps above, focusing on the traditional transition points between sales and marketing will often be the area of most change. Once the process of mapping, reviewing and suggesting is completed this can be passed up to the board for agreement, sign-off and communication approval to the wider organization.

Step 4 – The dynamic operating model

The final structure of the Smarketing organization and the processes that the organization runs are defined as the operating model. As this is being driven by the process outlined above, and engagement with customers is always changing, this needs to be based on a dynamic principal that allows change and adoption for the department and therefore, as the customer engagement engine, the business as a whole. To summarize this we want to outline that there are two types of operating model – the target operating model and the dynamic operating model. A short description of these follows.

The target operating model

The target operating model is a business state that is set for an extended period of time. This is normally done with a large and complex reorganization or change process that can take a long time. This means that the impact on the business cannot be repeated and the organization will keep this set operating approach for an extended period of time.

The dynamic operating model

The dynamic operating model takes an ongoing view to change and facilitates constant low-level change within the organization. The employees and processes must be able to cope with this and this is why the move to Smarketing offers the opportunity to change the operating model as well.

Figure 6.2 shows a visualization of the two models and the impact on the business.

Figure 6.2   How a target and dynamic operating model should function in an organization

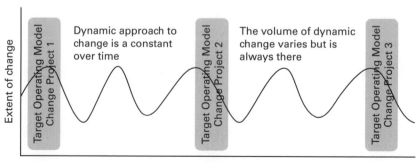

As the end-state organization is detailed this needs to be worked into processes, staff and ethos. We cannot highlight enough that in the modern fast-paced digital age the dynamic operating model is the only approach for the Smarketing department.

Step 5 – Sponsorship and buy-in

In the previous chapters we have discussed the importance of buy-in and the ways the Smarketing leader and the teams within the Smarketing department can go about communicating and acting effectively to achieve this. We will not repeat the points already made – we hope the importance of securing stakeholder buy-in is clear – but what we must do is just clarify some of the key determining factors that relate to this important issue. These might seem obvious points but for completeness we will clarifying below the core reasons for securing internal buy-in.

Why secure buy-in from other departments?

- **Support**: The Smarketing department does not stand alone in any organization and will always need support from the related business units; without a clear understanding of the new dynamic operating approach this is less likely.

- **Feedback**: Transforming in isolation means that there is limited feedback to the team and the leadership and this is vital, particularly from the board.

- **Understanding**: All parts of the business should have a good understanding of what Smarketing is, the steps to achieve it and also the challenges in achieving it, in order to support feedback.

- **Clarity**: All teams should have a clear view of the activity and the results of the Smarketing team, which may historically have been focused solely on the revenue figures. It is key that this is extended and communicated more widely and in detail to the management of the other main departments in the business.

In the following chapter we cover the reasons that transformation projects fail; in the case of Smarketing, with two such historically separate disciplines, the challenges and risks are great. We won't overemphasize this here, but will reinforce that this step of securing buy-in from the whole organization is vital to address it. With the right support and sponsorship, the team will have the necessary business momentum to succeed. One note on sponsorship is to highlight how vital it is as well. We have outlined the importance of a single leader within the Smarketing team but as part of this step that person must cement the sponsorship of key individuals in the organization. These should be members of the board and key influencers of that group, with roles such as the Chief Executive Officer, Head of Finance and leading non-executive board members being initial targets for full sponsorship. It can be very effective to have them involved in the communications and even day-to-day parts of the transformation. For example, giving their views on the impact of the transformation at all-hands meetings, or their own blog in any team newsletters, even just standing behind the Smarketing leader in any presentations or pictures can help to show their alignment, however subtle.

Additional to any groups outside of the Smarketing department this is the phase when the buy-in of the whole Smarketing project should be secured. The initial steps of this can be wider group engagement, via e-mails, video and presentations, but this has to move to as close to one-to-one as can be achieved depending on the company size. See it as a waterfall of the Smarketing leader securing the support of their management followed by those senior managers getting their teams' managers on board, all the way down to the front-line personnel in the organization. If every member of sales and marketing is talked to individually prior to starting the transformation project and understands the principles and objectives, the likelihood of success is much greater. The staff are then more likely to suggest ideas, volunteer and self-manage detractors themselves, helping to build the overall momentum to transformation at every level in the department.

We have touched on many ways to secure support, sponsorship and buy-in so here is a focused summary of the key approaches to achieving this:

- **Involve:** Bring people and teams into the process by making them part of relevant steps and outcomes. As outlined above this might be involvement in project teams.

- **Enable:** Help the rest of the business to understand via communication and training what Smarketing is and what will be different after the transformation project is complete.

- **Show:** Involve key stakeholders in the outcomes of the Smarketing team, whether it's customer success or team success.

- **Measure:** Provide complete end-to-end reports that give full visibility of the outcomes of the Smarketing team.

This is a key step that must not be missed and once established should be continued during the whole transformation and beyond.

Step 6 – Prove

The next step is to establish the reporting, measurement and governance of Smarketing. As touched on in the rest of the book this is a vital part of the process, without which failure to progress or change is guaranteed. As such we have devoted Chapter 8 to cover this more fully. Here it is worth detailing that the use of these reports as proof of progress is part of this step. Once the reporting is established, regular use of the reports to communicate to the various parts of the business will help with all the steps detailed in this chapter, specifically the buy-in, support and sponsorship that this programme will need to succeed.

However, to start your understanding and prepare you for that chapter here are some of the key points:

- Measurements down the whole customer engagement funnel without breaks or changes in the process of reporting with a single team providing the numbers.

- Moving to view the engagement of each entire company that you work with rather than focusing on single points of engagement. In effect, moving from person-based to company-based customer reporting.

- Remuneration of teams to be rationalized against these two reporting fundamentals with visibility of this to all teams, encouraging openness on bonus structures.

In Chapter 8 we will talk about the importance of showing the results in a connected way, breaking down the silos and therefore joining up the customer experience.

Step 7 – Compensate

Following on from measurement is the step to determine the approach to remuneration. Historically the sales and marketing departments have had very different remuneration, with telemarketing sitting in the middle when it comes to the weighting of base salary to bonus. It is well known that remuneration drives behaviour and as such this is a key step to get right in order to change the customer experience.

When setting the compensation of the Smarketing teams the values should be clearly set to increase the quality of the customer experience. As such, during the journey-mapping process this needs to be factored in as well. Not the value, but possible existing payment proportions or base salary vs bonus payment and what might work better. Obviously, testing may be required and this is not something that can be done in a mock environment as the actual manifestations of human nature will take time and reality to expose. This is also something that can cause staff erosion if not handled well; no one wants to have the 'goalposts' constantly changing or to not reach a target for a bonus because it was not available for long enough. As such, this is something that must be evaluated carefully and implemented in a phased way over extended periods of time.

In reviewing the approach to remuneration across the departments, moving to a tiering that flows alongside the customer engagement cycle is an evolved version of current bonus to basic schemes often seen in marketing. Figures 6.3 to 6.5 outline how the evolution to Smarketing compensation might occur; this gives a view of the changes in remuneration.

Figure 6.3 Employees are typically compensated in two types of salary and bonus scenarios

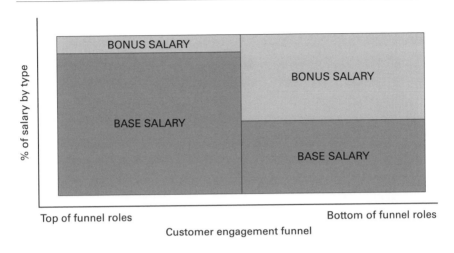

Figure 6.4 In a Smarketing world, employees may need to be paid with more varied mechanisms covering salary and bonus

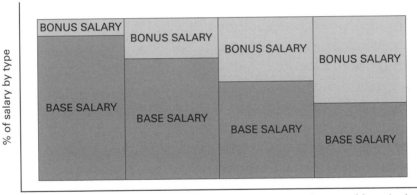

Overall, changing the culture to one of transparency and participation will come from changing the remuneration to a more evenly stepped approach. Having a close clarity of view on the next team in how they are remunerated will only help to develop this culture, and this will be passed on to customers in the way that staff engage. It is always obvious to customers when there are unhappy staff and

Figure 6.5   Salary and bonus needs to be in tune with the business as well as the customer's objectives

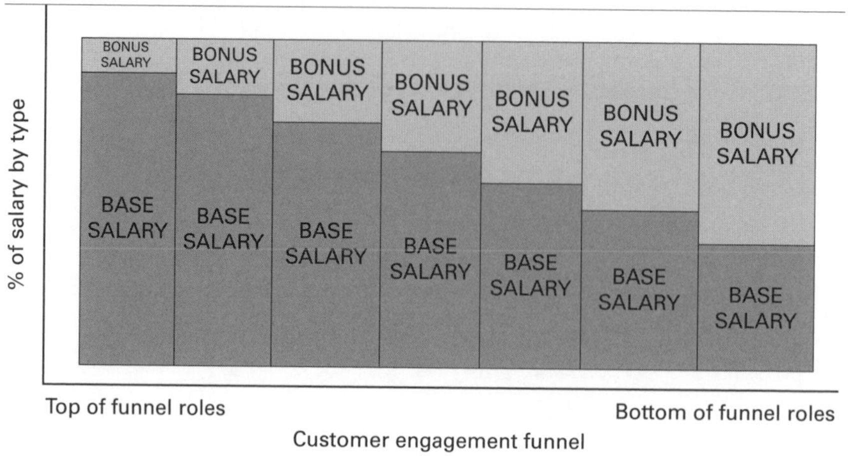

Top of funnel roles   Bottom of funnel roles

Customer engagement funnel

reducing the number of these via the right compensation is important to the success of Smarketing.

The big challenge in all of this is managing the costs; this must be closely monitored to prevent them spiralling out of control when changing too many remuneration packages during the transformation. As we show above, moving to clarity on the percentage levels does not need to relate to any actual salaries but gives an indicator to the other teams of how a person is incentivized. This in turn helps them to understand how best to work with that person.

It may be that in the short term, large bonus packages are redistributed across teams to start this move, and then as the financial impact is better understood, but this needs to be closely managed across the whole process. The key here is to avoid any negative impact, so work with staff to secure the right outcome with limited impact and, if in doubt, delay compensation changes with new staff as there is nothing more sensitive than this.

Step 8 – Start and extend

The final step, after all the above preparation, is to kick off the transformation proper and drive the value to your customers. With the right support, both from within sales and marketing and the rest of the business, the excitement of moving to a fundamentally new model should be there across every individual. This is really the time for all to shine and show how they can adapt to the new working approach and succeed in an environment that is providing a better customer experience. This should mean that the customers themselves are better engaged with the various teams. Obviously, for the new engagements nothing changes at the very first touchpoints, but as every step after that is optimized their propensity to progress with your organization should only increase and multiply.

The keys to success in delivering will vary but the following are common irrespective of the type or size of business:

- First, focus on the historic gaps in the customer engagement cycle. From the journey mapping take the major issues and 'pinch points' and address those. This doesn't cover everything equally, but prioritize and focus.

- Second, bring the whole organization together on the process: transparency is key. Communication and visibility of all that is going on will drive success. In the UK there was a period when members of parliament were becoming more and more distrusted and one element of this was the perception the public paid for everything for them. As such, the government started to publish the expense claims of its cabinet members and soon any MP not publishing theirs was ridiculed and not voted for. Despite some notable news stories relating to this the objective of re-establishing the support of the public was achieved. Bear this example in mind with your business and consider how internal openness with other departments can fundamentally drive buy-in, support and unity in the business.

- Third, work through all the senior management to drive a culture of empowerment through change. This transformation, as outlined with the dynamic operating model, is a constant and should not be seen as a simple target end state. It will need a cultural shift to embrace this, which the leadership must drive.

- Fourth (and finally), find and activate any detractors. We have touched on this previously in the book but want to highlight this again as vital to success.

Conclusion

Overall this transformation will be major and taking a stepped approach is the only way to achieve success. Following the outline above and always focusing will help to drive that change. Working with your external stakeholders to sanity-check the progress and the impact will also help of course to adjust, refocus and incentivize with any successes. As the transformation progresses, finding customer success stories that can be used internally will help everyone to understand tangibly how their experiences have changed.

A key thing for the Smarketing leader to bear in mind during this transformation is the velocity of the change. It is well documented in business that this is a key challenge and can be a limiting factor. Change too fast and the business can suffer, change too slow and the end state is not reached in a timeframe that is meaningful. Focusing on the key areas that we outline will help, and as touched on Chapter 8, with reporting, measurement and governance, some points of change can almost happen without change to the actual structure or personnel.

Questions to ask yourself

1 If one of your core team was stopped in the lift/elevator by one of your employees and challenged about the Smarketing programme, could they clearly articulate (quickly) the benefits and the direction of travel of the programme?

2 Have the programme benefits and timescale been clearly communicated to all stakeholders and employees, and have any objections, concerns and suggestions been collated, documented and fed back into the programme?

3 Are you clear that all employees impacted have had a one-to-one discussion and that they are clear in terms of their role, the benefit to them and the company, and the impact on their employee terms and conditions?

4 What is your plan to keep management and employees continually informed, and how will you make sure that this doesn't distract you from the day-to-day tasks? Will you employee a PMO (Programme Management Officer)? This is a department (or a person) within a business that supports, defines and maintains standards for project management. The PMO has responsibility for governance and report of the project. The objective is to free up the project manager and other project members.

5 Are you on target to reach your goals and stretch them? Do you have quick wins you can communicate out?

Challenges of Smarketing and how to overcome them

07

In Chapter 4 we switched from a 'why' to a 'how'; the whole point of this book is not to preach to you but to offer a practical approach so that you can chart a course and strategy in the waters of this new internet-enabled world. But it would be wrong for us (to continue the nautical metaphor) to suggest that this is going to be plain sailing: it isn't. There will be many barriers and blockers to overcome if you are to stand a chance of successfully implementing Smarketing. It requires a change to your organization and change is hard. Smarketing is not a dream. Smarketing is a process and a structure that is applicable to your business, whatever the size and complexity. Smarketing is not out of your reach but that said, Smarketing is going to be a difficult concept for your organization to embrace.

Clearly, having a strategy for how to implement a Smarketing methodology (or structure) is going to be crucial for you but so is finding a weight of evidence that builds a business case for embarking on the journey – we are hoping that this book will help you with both of those challenges.

Some of the key barriers that you are likely to encounter are listed in the following pages, as are some strategies which might help you to overcome those particular roadblocks.

As this book provides a practical methodology for you to implement Smarketing in your organization, it is only right and proper that we itemize some of the blockers you will find and offer a suggested plan for you to work your way around. No project is risk-free, but we can at least lower the risk.

There is an old proverb: 'forewarned is forearmed'.

Feeling the pain

Every business is different and each enterprise has differing levels of success in its current sales and marketing processes. Irrespective of that, one of the biggest agents of change within any business is pain. In our 'day job' at Digital Leadership Associates, we are often approached by clients who are at their wits' end. Their company is simply unable to sell their products or services into the modern marketplace in the way that they used to be able to; the pain has reached unbearable levels and the business is looking for a solution. If you are in this situation, driving change will be much easier than if the business is stable. The pain needs alleviating and Smarketing could be the solution. This isn't saying, of course, that being against the ropes is a good situation to be in, but the business will have seen in a very straightforward and visceral way that the current practices aren't working and that they will need to do something, perhaps something radical, to deal with the issue. The impetus, you could say, will already be there.

By contrast, if you are working in a flourishing environment, driving change will be much more of a challenge. We know from our own experiences that when businesses have full pipelines and a good margin on their products and services there is not only no imperative to change but the full risk of change is crystallized. The answer, 'well we can't be doing too much wrong as we're exhibiting strong growth year on year' will most likely be the response. There is a saying that it is easier to fix your roof when it's sunny, but as we have often seen in business, this is not always the case.

That's fine: perhaps your business isn't ready for Smarketing yet... or perhaps it is!

The reality of the situation is that the history books are littered with organizations that have been in a strong, sometimes preeminent position, sometimes for decades, then those organizations have been forced out in a very short time. Afraid of the risks involved in making changes to the status quo they have been exploiting for years, they have not seen that the risk is in fact not the risk of change, but the risk of standing still and being overtaken by the competition.

In an earlier chapter we quoted Capgemini's tweet saying that 52 per cent of the Fortune 500 companies present in the year 2000 are now gone. These were the largest, most stable, most profitable organizations that simply were not well enough adapted to be able to change with their market and more importantly their customers' needs.

So, highlighting that the risk involved in not embracing these new techniques is arguably one of the bigger risks in the modern business world is a key move for you. You will need to find a way of building a sense of desire and a sense of motivation to change in an organization that possibly shows all the signs of being a success, with no spectre of change and no fresh new dynamic on the horizon in your space. Nobody said this was going to be easy though!

Buy-in to the concept

The idea of Smarketing will have many naysayers in any organization. People who don't believe that it can work. People who don't understand what the purpose of it is. People who fear that this may invalidate their own hard-won position (and compensation) within the organization as it stands.

As with the previous 'building the pain' point, you will probably need to begin sewing seeds for how the benefits of change could be significant, and the risks of not embracing these new ideas equally significant.

As is often the case in organizations, change is accompanied by fear and, as with a round of redundancies, the narrative often begins with the line, 'we are determined to safeguard all jobs…'

There will in this situation be winners and losers, so identifying who the probable champions are within the organization will be paramount to your success. The problem is that both sales and marketing are likely to want to be in overall control of this programme (unless they are like Rhiannon Prothero, Marketing Director at SAP, who is more concerned about the customer experience than being in overall control of the programme and the result) and therefore your buy-in may not necessarily need to start in either of these departments.

Organization structure usually (but not always) means that the further up the organization you look, the more strategic their view of the organization becomes. Sales and marketing, certainly at an operational level, tend to view the world on a quarter-by-quarter (or campaign-by-campaign) basis. This is understandable and actually necessary from an operational perspective, but you probably need to be looking elsewhere to find your champions.

If you can speak to one of the C-suite (or directors) that will be a good starting point because they will have more influence and will possibly have a longer-term view of the proceedings. Whoever it is that you find, you will need to very clearly articulate what the benefits of moving to a Smarketing model are and what's in it for them. Anyone who pushes this programme, irrespective of its success or failure, will be risking political capital in doing so and consequently they will want to see a 'personal win' for them in this. Financial? Promotion? Kudos? Something great on their CV? Whatever their motivation may be, you will need to clearly push those buttons as they may be putting their neck on the line.

Power bases

Having worked in medium and large enterprises it's easy to see that there are various power bases: head of sales, board/C-suite, HR, operations, marketing. Often these people and departments are vying for supremacy. Usually this isn't for any apparent reason other than ego. They rarely (with a few exceptions) cross paths but they sometimes want to make sure that their voice is the one that counts.

Making sure that you have the right backing amongst those that either wield the power or perhaps have influence over those that do, could well be a good tactic for getting the job done.

You need to make sure that not only does your proposal for Smarketing get the backing it deserves (and needs) but that those backing it are vocal enough that it is on the agenda at the important meetings where it should be discussed.

Like getting the right sponsorship, these powerbrokers will be important to you in pushing the change through. These people need to see the long-term benefits or objectives of the Smarketing programme and understand how they can 'sell this' to others within the organization. These powerbroker people often have a desire to make a difference within an organization even if they are not necessarily the recipient of the benefit of that difference.

Perhaps a good book to read prior to starting your quest would be *The Prince*, by Niccolò Machiavelli; it's a good grounding in strategic politics and you may well need a dose of that!

Short-term vs long-term thinking

As mentioned above, one of the big challenges that you are going to need to overcome is the short-term objectives (and therefore thinking) of middle management and the long-term objectives (and therefore thinking) of senior management.

Sales and marketing managers (and directors) are often measured and incentivized on quarterly targets – sales figures, campaign success, pipeline, whatever it may be – and the requirement to keep churning out what may at a strategic level be rather pointless results and metrics takes nothing away from the fact that those are the figures that determine whether the person keeps or loses their job.

To interfere with this process and therefore the ability of them to be able to generate their own personal success will mean that many people will try to throw out the idea of adopting a different model before it gets off the ground.

From inside experience we know how salespeople, for example, are driven by incentives in what they sell and how they sell it. I know of one occasion where the sales lead sold a product that the client neither needed nor wanted because at the time that product carried a higher sales commission than the products that would have been useful. This might seem a rather short-term view of proceedings, and of course it is, but in an environment where even successful salespeople's response to the question 'how are you?' is often 'well I haven't been sacked yet' shows that many times it is the tactical approach that has the bigger bearing on actions

So once again, it will fall to you to identify within your organization not just who should be your champion and who are the power brokers, but who is likely to have a more strategic and long-term view of what needs to happen.

Clearly, talking to someone who is in a panic about making their quarter three (Q3) quota about how a two-year programme to help sales and marketing departments to be more closely aligned operationally and objectively is likely to fall on deaf ears.

Organizational inertia

Probably the biggest of the issues you will face though is organizational inertia. This is a challenge to any sort of change within a large enterprise, or even a medium-sized business. This will be doubly difficult if your business hasn't struggled to make sales so far, or to put it another way, there is no pain being felt.

Even if you manage to get buy-in and build a groundswell of opinion at each level of the organization and have managed to align all of the powerbrokers, the stakeholders, the champions and the strategic thinkers that you need, the inertia encountered when getting people to change their thinking and behaviours organization-wide will sometimes seem like an insurmountable barrier to overcome.

We at Digital Leadership Associates see this every day. A hugely successful pilot programme and absolute proof of success does not necessarily mean that a transformation will take off, as organizational inertia will conspire to stop the process of change. Partly this will be due to many people simply not feeling the same degree of desire about the project as you do, and partly it will be down to many people not caring, but you will also need to have a strategy to deal with the more vocal objectors to change.

The inertia Venn diagram in business shows that some of the key factors that affect an individual within the organization's propensity to change are fear, power and competition (both internal and external).

Figure 7.1   Corporate inertia © Digital Leadership Associates

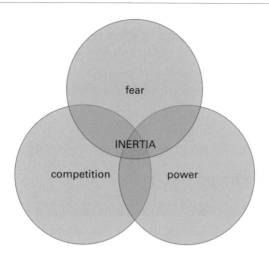

The truth is that getting such a 'radical' concept adopted will likely be met with resistance at every step of the way. Of course, I'm not saying that Smarketing is in any way a radical concept. On the contrary, it makes perfect sense, but many people won't see it that way, despite the fact that the challenges that are overcome by deploying Smarketing as a concept within your business are enormous. The way that Smarketing delivers on-the-ground benefits to sales teams that manifest themselves in increased fame, inbound leads and revenue rather than such intangible things as viability, share of voice or impressions should help you to construct a good rationale for this way of thinking. However, you will need to bear in mind that you are asking people who allocate budgets (but may not really understand marketing) to completely reposition what they think a marketing function within a business should look like and you are asking people in the marketing department to radically change what they do now.

Where might resistance be?

Consider where you should expect the resistance to come from and what you think you should do about it. Identifying what the drivers for each of those areas of resistance might be and creating an argument to nullify them is always a good plan.

So, who or where might resistance come from, why might they be resistant, what are their objectives and how can Smarketing help them achieve them? What are the risks of them backing a Smarketing programme in the organization? We will now look at the different areas of resistance you might find and explain a recommendation you might follow.

SVPs and the board or C-suite

The senior management will probably have a pretty damn good understanding of the operational peculiarities of the business. They may well be aware of which areas within the business are working efficiently and which are not; however, we all know that compensation drives behaviour and the C-suite is no different.

Despite having what is ostensibly a strategic role, many senior people still think in quite a tactical short-term way. They are answerable to the shareholders or the stock market and often these groups are only interested in quarter-on-quarter growth. The C-suite are often compensated on this basis too, and therefore whatever happens tomorrow is less important than what happens today.

But that shouldn't stop you from creating a 'playbook' for the C-suite. They need convincing that this is the right move like everyone else does. Changes in buyer behaviour and old sales paradigms not holding true should be a powerful message for them and one that won't have gone unnoticed already. The fact that their helicopter view of the business validates everything you will be telling them should support your assertion that sales and marketing need to have a closer and more efficient relationship.

The short-term benefit for them could be that it will enable the business to field a higher return on investment (ROI) from this new kind of set-up. Stripping cost and complexity out of the business is always something that appeals the top management. The removal of large-scale (and large-cost) campaigns in favour of more structured targeted ones should find favour, and the fact that the structure you're proposing will mean a massive uplift in efficiency, with marketing teams being more focused on the needs of the sales teams at a tactical level whilst still providing the strategic thrusts into specific industries and verticals, should, with luck, be a compelling message.

If you can join the dots in their minds so that they can see that setting up these two departments to be more efficient and productive in this way not only delivers a short-term revenue benefit but also makes the company stronger in the long term, this should help them to see that this is a game with minimal risk and one which not only supports their short-term personal KPIs but also sets them up for a long-term future in the company through being an agent of change and helping to future-proof the organization.

Sales

Within the medium-to-small enterprise (MSE) space, in companies with a turnover (T/O) of less than £500 million/$800 million, marketing and sales can often be quite aligned, in fact almost running Smarketing already. But as the organization gets larger, the siloed nature of these departments means that division is almost inevitable. There is the cultural divide; salespeople tend to look at marketers as wage slaves with secure jobs. They also can see marketers as subordinates who do their bidding – I need a brochure for this, or I need an event for these people, or I need more leads or whatever catcall sticking plaster is required.

Sales, in my experience, actually quite like this and this in itself might be a barrier to deploying Smarketing within the organization. Sales still largely live in the *Glengarry Glen Ross* world of machismo closers going into battle with their foes (clients) and forcing the deal. In the real world this isn't how things actually are any more, but salespeople often like to believe that they are. In Digital Leadership Associates we have an extremely good salesperson who, despite the fact that he goes above and beyond the call of duty with all of his clients, comes back to the office and replays lines from *Jerry Maguire* and *Tin Men*!

> ### Rhiannon Prothero – Marketing Director UK & Ireland, SAP
>
> ... we might be super-efficient in our telemarketing operation, but if it's not the right thing for this customer we should not do it and we have to break process and that's really the nuts of it, knowing when to break process to deliver a better experience or an appropriate experience.

Whilst this is quite good fun and always raises a laugh it does highlight the point that salespeople like to be in control, partly of course because they can never be in control of the sale (as the client is) and partly because they just love to be the centre of attention.

Breaking down those walls between sales and marketing moves them into the same ball park as each other and this will always find resistance from the [superior] salespeople.

So, understanding these behavioural traits should make negotiating with them a little easier.

Salespeople probably won't like the idea that marketing are taking on what might be considered a more hands-on or even a more strategic role in the relationship, but they probably will be very happy that marketing will be more reactive to their needs. Having help to facilitate the right tools at the right place at the right time so they can over-achieve their quota is going to be a pleasing prospect for every salesperson. This majors on the fact that salespeople are 'up against it' and that marketing in this new role will be much more empowered to help salespeople close business rather than just organization campaigns which, for many salespeople, don't seem to do much to deliver pipeline, and certainly not pipeline which closes.

Operations

Within every organization there is an 'operations' department and their role has been to look for efficiencies and to create replicable processes for when the company expands. So you would imagine that this would be right up their street as this is a huge potential efficiency.

Possibly not, though. Operations will have a 'best practice' book which will have been created over decades, often by some of the best brains on the consulting world, and Smarketing is a chapter in this book which will be noticeably absent.

Whilst it's probable that the operations department won't have much sway in strategic matters such as whether Smarketing is implemented or not, like all departments (and people) that might have a voice, it's probably worth talking them through what the benefits are and what their role is likely to be (or at least any possible impact on them).

Whilst they may see this as the creation of an entirely new series of workflows and processes, it probably isn't going to be that. There will of course need to be new workflow, but the foundations for them at a macro level will already be there and at a micro level little will probably change. Content creation, design, legal will all happen largely as they do already.

For the operations department though, as with every other department, being involved in a transformation which delivers reduced cost, increased results and a better dialogue between two large functions within the business is an opportunity to gain some significant kudos.

Marketing

Marketing themselves! I know that it's rather ironic that when you offer a lifebelt to a drowning person they might choose not to take it, but the marketing department will be one of the biggest challenges you will need to overcome.

People who have chosen marketing as a career and have perhaps studied for a diploma or even a degree in it have, in my experience, had their ability to innovate programmed out of them. If they are good, they will validate all of their decisions with data, but often they aren't able to step back from the situation and think about what else that data might be suggesting as opposed to what they WANT it to suggest. The idea that the marketing department, with its clear career progression and (if we are being brutal) often absence of accountability, would voluntarily give this up in favour of joining the sales department on the front line is a big leap.

One problem is that the marketing function simply doesn't value what sales does (which is ironic because the sales function doesn't value what marketing does) because in marketing's eyes sales is simply a bunch of people who close business by forcing customers (who marketing have already groomed) to buy products they would have bought anyway. In the eyes of the marketer the salesperson has tenacity but little skill or education.

The idea for the marketer that they will be working hand-in-hand with sales is probably not particularly appealing and possibly quite scary. This is in part because of this lack of understanding of what sales does and in part because the marketer knows that instead of having a career where they can plan three, four, five years ahead they will be moving into an environment where they will be living on their wits, quarter by quarter.

This lack of understanding on the side of marketing and the fear of what an almost-sales role might hold will create a huge backlash... even though the rationale is straightforward and easy to justify.

Another potential problem is that the inertia within a marketing department to a new technology or campaign being adopted is inversely proportional to how 'sexy' that campaign or project is. Everyone in marketing wants to be involved in sponsorship and TV advertising; nobody wants to be involved in newsletters and blogging, even though blogging will arguably provide a far higher ROI than some of the cooler projects.

Figure 7.2   Inertia increases exponentially with sexiness!

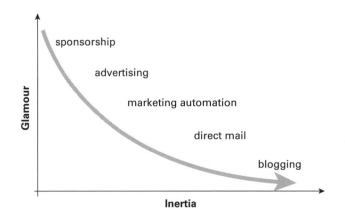

So, the question is, 'is Smarketing seen as a glamorous enough idea to truly appeal to marketers?'

The marketer more than anyone will be aware of changes in behaviour amongst the public. Be they B2B or B2C they will have seen the effectiveness of their various campaigns reduce each year. They will have also seen the predictability of their campaigns disappear. They have seen their customers (or perhaps targets) become more and more elusive over time as they have failed to angle either the head or the heart of those individuals and they are now painted into a corner where they have been largely disempowered as a business function. The glory days of glamorous big-budget TV commercials and the ability to create more demand than the factory can fulfil have largely disappeared, to be replaced by simply carrying out a hygiene function. This means that they have largely lost the respect of the rest of the business in many cases. Tim (co-author of the book) sometimes teasingly refers to marketing as 'the colouring-in department', and whilst this is said without any trace of malice it does underline how sales feel about the emasculated marketing department of the modern corporation.

Marketing, though, is more critically aware than any other department of how the shifts in buying behaviour, or perhaps more accurately the shift in researching suppliers, are affecting businesses on a day-to-day basis. Marketing, the department that once held all the aces is now struggling to find its relevance in the modern organization and the adoption of Smarketing is its opportunity to restore relevance and direction rather than simply going through the motions.

Of course, this new-found purpose and the amazing opportunity afforded by Smarketing for the marketing department is absolutely no guarantee whatsoever that marketing will grasp this with both hands, so the sale of this idea will have to be handled with some sensitivity and be well crafted to succeed.

If after answering the questions below you have a clear idea of who you need to get on side and you have a feeling that the organization is not going to 'flat-out refuse' to entertain the idea of Smarketing then this might be a possibility and certainly one that you should be considering.

Politics

Of course, reading through this chapter you might think that making this transformation happen is more a matter of politics than it is a matter of change, or merging, or strategy, and to a certain extent it is.

In every business (other than micro-businesses) there is a big gulf between what makes sense and can benefit the organization and what actually gets done. This isn't, we stress, because there is any malicious intent by anyone who is simply seeking to block the development of the organization, it is more about ensuring that everyone understands what the benefits are and how the journey is going to take place.

The key to this is going to be making sure that everyone is saying the same things about the importance of the transformation and the shared vision of what Smarketing could offer to the business.

Are you ready for this?

If you don't feel that this is something that your organization is ready for yet, before discounting it you might want to think again.

We said at the very beginning that this is a big ask of both you and the organization. We also said that organizational change is one of the most difficult things to achieve because humans are creatures of habit and forming new habits is extremely difficult, and this will require a large number of people to change.

However, the pot of gold at the end of this rainbow is certainly one that is worth looking for. What we know for certain is that neither sales nor marketing are working in their current forms. If you consider the mobile phone company Vodafone in the UK, they have almost no sales force. What they have is a (rare) powerful marketing department which creates enough noise in the marketplace that all prospective customers know who they are. They then have an effective enough conversion tool in their website that people either buy online or go into the stores to sign the paperwork. Either way, the salesforce has largely been reduced to shop staff. Is that what you want for your company? Equally, do you want marketing to be replaced by an outsourced corporate brochure website and a rival sales team that create their own materials on the fly? Again, no, of course you don't.

So, if that's how you feel it's important that you get on the Smarketing journey and be the one driving this forward, or at least on the team that are, because this is very clearly where the future lies.

Conclusion

Failing to plan is planning to fail. To push any change through the organization it is imperative to have a plan. Identifying which individuals and departments are resistant to this change will be a valuable exercise in the long run. Getting those people on side and ensuring that they are fully versed in the importance (and the potential glory) of this will be very beneficial.

There is an old saying 'change is exciting when it happens to someone else...' so making sure that everyone who a Smarketing transformation touches fully buys in to it is going to be helpful. As is the recognition that whilst the long-term objective of Smarketing is 'sexy', the work and processes in the short term, like with any change programme, are as far from sexiness as you can get!

Overall though it's best to recognize that building a groundswell of opinion and belief in the change, whilst being difficult, will be an awful lot easier than single-handedly trying to pull the whole enterprise behind you on this journey.

Questions to ask yourself

1 Is your organization ready for Smarketing?

2 What is going to stop you achieving your goals?

3 What are the risks?

4 What can you be doing now to overcome them?

5 Who should you get on side to support, champion and promote this programme internally?

Reference

Capgemini Consulting (2015) When digital disruption strikes: How can incumbents respond (Published on Twitter 10 May 2015 – 6:25 pm) [Last accessed 16 May 2018]

Measurement, reporting and governance

08

The greatest danger in times of turbulence is not the turbulence – it is to act with yesterday's logic.
PETER DRUCKER

Introduction

As we have touched on in the other chapters the importance of measurement, reporting and governance is paramount. As we will conclude at the end of this chapter there is nothing more important to the process of Smarketing than getting these things right. When you think about all the points that we have covered, all of this is underpinned by the measurement you have and the ability to clearly communicate against that measurement. In any organization, no matter the type, being able to understand the data in front of you underpins your, and the entity's, ability to make decisions. Across the professional world many decisions are made by human interpretation often based on 'gut feel' and this is something that today modern business needs to avoid.

There is nothing more vital than substantiated decision making with individuals empowered by the information they have available to them. We can all list the organizations that have failed over the years and it has often been clear that financial understanding within the organization has not been effective enough. There have been organizations of all sizes that have suffered from this and have disappeared as a result, but we are of the strong opinion that it is not just the financial reporting that is at fault. For the other departments to abdicate any responsibility for the understanding of the imminent demise of any organization is not good enough. This is where Smarketing and the rigour that comes with effective, useful and insightful reporting comes in. One of the fundamental objectives of Smarketing is to provide the understanding that can help steer the business well in advance of any financial challenges.

A simple analogy for this would be for any business reviewing its web traffic; where they see significant decline it would be expected that there will be less overall interest in the company at the following steps in engagement, which ultimately means less revenue. If an organization has the right visibility and understanding, then action can be taken early, and this is what Smarketing needs to deliver. In this chapter we will outline the reasoning and approaches to get your house in order to deliver the right reports to allow the right measurement and governance.

Smarketing is driven by measurement

The speed of decision making is the essence of good governance.

PIYUSH GOYAL

Once we accept that Smarketing cannot happen without the right governance you need to start the process to move towards evolving the information that you as an organization have available and the breadth of that information. As touched on in Chapter 6, this is one of the main steps we see in moving to modern Smarketing. At the outset of this key step, having a clear vision of the end state will provide a goal against which to measure your progress. This goal should be simple and straightforward and agreed between the Smarketing leadership and particularly with the Smarketing leader. To that end, focusing on the end-to-end reporting should be the aim, and the goal for reporting should clearly stipulate that it should:

- deliver agreed consistent reporting across the whole customer engagement cycle;
- additionally there may well be some ancillary direction for the team;

- allow all solutions or products to have their engagement with customers measured;
- drive any remuneration for any team engaging customers at any point in the process;
- facilitate customer insight based on intent characteristics from your first-party data.

With a clear goal established and agreed it will fall to the operations leadership to then take this forward and deliver against this goal.

We have talked about the importance of unifying the operations teams to have a single Smarketing operations team and this is the big driver for doing this. Without a unified team there is little hope of having a single agreed reporting view that can deliver the types of insight and analysis organizations need today.

There are three parts to the team that need to come together to deliver the Smarketing operations team:

1 **Marketing operations**: The team that supports marketing and traditionally are responsible for the marketing-oriented elements of the CRM (customer relationship management) system. Marketing operations will often have reporting in place for various dimensions of analysis that may or may not be shared with the wider organization. This reporting often ends at the step where some form of marketing qualified lead is generated and this is seen as the 'output' from marketing.

2 **Sales enablement**: The team that supports the skills and capabilities of the sales organization has a huge wealth of insight and information about the actual business practices and should be a key part of the Smarketing operations team. Delivering the enablement out to the whole team including marketing will secure more value from the combined teams, as traditionally this team does not support enabling marketing as well.

3 **Sales operations**: This team often focuses on pipeline reporting and very much the metrics at the bottom of the customer engagement cycle. In many businesses these are seen as the most important metrics and are provided by sales leadership to finance and the board.

Taking these teams and joining them together will deliver many positive impacts, the key one being visibility along the whole customer engagement cycle. As touched on above, traditionally sales numbers are often delivered in isolation, covering very much the bottom of the engagement funnel, with other metrics above not being aligned or seen as impacting these numbers. However, the reality is the relationship is intrinsically linked and change at any earlier stage in customer engagement that will have a knock-on effect further down the cycle.

Evolved reporting and measurement

The legacy of sales and marketing being different disciplines has meant that over the years the reporting and information for each have also become separated. As many reading this book from either side of the Smarketing house will no doubt be aware, during any professional training or education there are extensive modules, classes or books on both. Certainly when we trained in our various disciplines of sales and marketing we remember sitting through hours of detailed explanation of marketing reporting and the importance of the marketing qualified lead. It was in the practical execution of marketing that the issues with passing these to a separated sales team came into effect, with a constant drive to avoid the 'throwing it over the wall' approach to marketing leads. Whether this was ever really addressed remains to be seen but I am sure that in every organization both sales and marketing professionals can attest to this issue. From the sales side sentiments around marketing leads are definitely varied and in some instances no doubt not entirely positive. The main issue is simply that the process and reporting are split and no matter the intent, the lack of understanding that this causes underpins the concern with sales and marketing today.

The marketing department measuring at varying levels, from the initial contact with a customer to the generation of a marketing qualified lead or similar marketing output, and then sales measuring from the receipt of those leads down to close, is a common story. Even to get to the point that each department has a clear understanding

Figure 8.1 Consolidate the funnel

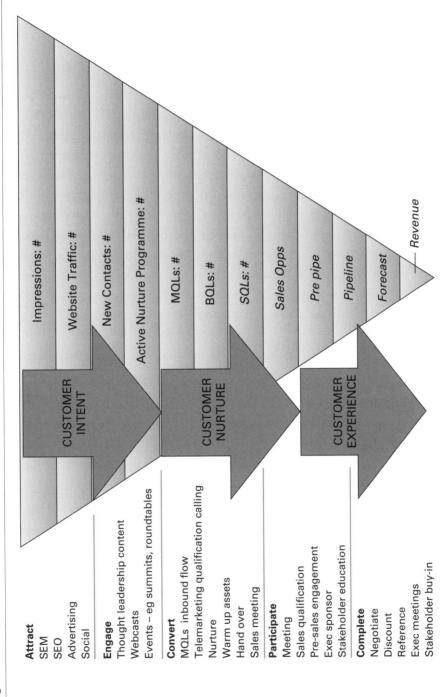

of its whole 'funnel' is rare, and reporting and measurement, often driven by company revenue objectives and compensation plans, is normally patchy. To compound this, it can be that different teams in the same department have different details to their reports and use different terminology to articulate progress and success. And all this is compounded the larger and more complex the organization.

For Smarketing to work we have to move to full reporting for the business down the whole customer engagement cycle, from web traffic to closed business, delivered by a single operations team.

Another vital part of this process is to align the nomenclature of the reporting that Smarketing uses. Moving to a single agreed set of terms that are clearly understood or referenceable is essential. This can then be communicated in every report, in the CRM system and via the enablement team so that the Smarketing team and also the wider business build out that understanding and common approach. It means that even if there are different teams doing different things the measurement approach can be common, giving a simpler view when combined across multiple business units. The old saying of 'comparing apples with apples' sums up the intent here.

If this single view is achieved there are some clear outcomes that will be delivered as a result:

- **Business alignment**: Having all parts of the organization with the same view that can be consolidated for the senior Smarketing management drives consistency across the business and specifically alignment through the ability to compare departments against a standard view.

- **Single reporting view**: The efficiency of a single centrally created view is another outcome, saving the time taken creating individual reports. The value to all in decision making will become apparent quickly as the interpretation of the information evolves as well.

- **Standard terminology**: This is needed to provide like-for-like comparison, and underpins the transformation to single reporting view.

- **Benchmark evaluation**: With a single view across the customer engagement cycle it becomes possible to review certain steps and deep-dive into the process and departments against industry benchmarks to understand what is good and where things need to change.

- **Intent analysis**: An objective to determine intent from your first-party data is absolutely vital. We will touch more on this later in this chapter, but moving to a single view by customer or prospect company will facilitate this.

More than just the numbers

In building a single operations team there are many other tasks that this team needs to undertake alongside the vital role of delivering these end-to-end reports. They can also drive and support any compliance commitments that the organization needs to meet such as the ubiquitous General Data Protection Regulation (GDPR) or other more specific regulations for your industry. Having a department built around common practice and insight will also facilitate any of these commitments. In all of this the single leader of the operations will be the vital unifying role to define the scope of the team and the support that they can give.

One element that can be highly effective, especially when aiming for a dynamic operating model, is to have a sub-team within operations that can take on any project. This project management office is the equivalent of a special forces unit in the military, deployed for focused key tasks that cannot be carried out by or would distract the main force. Having such a team allows for the fast and effective carrying out of tests of business processes or approaches. As a sub-team, being familiar with working across the organization means they can build small teams to try new products, open new offices, deploy new systems or just run new analysis of existing data from the centralized reports.

The scale and focus of this team depends on the size of the business but at the very least having someone or a part of a person to lead these projects is vital to actually delivering a dynamic business. The reason for this is that any special project is always at the whim of staff's day job and the bandwidth they have. This is the main factor in the failure of special projects, and having dedicated bandwidth in the organization to cover this facilitates agility, which in our fast-paced world, is vital.

Changing the view

At the heart of the change to Smarketing is a move from a siloed view of your market engagement to a much more holistic view. This needs to be delivered by viewing the way your organization interacts in markets differently, and will underpin your ability to get an intent-based view of your market from your own first-party data. Simply put, for any B2B-focused entity, having a single view of the companies you are engaging is the target approach to reporting. The aim is to move away from looking at any individual metrics such as leads attached to decision makers, and towards to a holistic view for each business you are engaged with.

This approach is not new but is hard to achieve as legacy process and also systems are often transactionally focused so do not inherently provide that cross-business view. For complex businesses with multiple divisions or products this becomes even more important and drives the success of the overall customer experience and customer engagement. An analogy to help illustrate the issue is one we have probably all been through in the insurance industry. A number of years ago the holy grail of insurance was to solve the multi-channel challenge and most insurers have now made this change in how they engage their customers and prospects. The issue they used to have was that each division of the business delivered a slightly different customer experience and often the actual information on each customer was not shared. As a customer we didn't care about these internal challenges, we just wanted to know that the letter we might have sent was also referenced in any telephone conversation we might have and that our online account was updated with any outcomes agreed on the phone. This was not always the case and after much change insurers addressed the issue to provide their internal teams with a single customer view. In many instances we have a single view of the customer now but we do not reflect this in the reporting and certainly not across the whole customer engagement cycle.

So, the aim of the Smarketing operations team is to deliver this view for each target business or account and thereby generate referenceable value for each target account. This is the start of an account engagement score (AES) or account intent value.

Account engagement score (AES)

This value should take into account all the touchpoints from which the business has accrued a value based on the weighting of each engagement to provide a single score by account. This should be built up from all the first-party data available, from web visit via domain tracking all the way to individual sales opportunities. This will allow the business to view the marketplace based on this common score, and with cross-referenced data will highlight the best areas in which to focus your teams. The aim here is to look at the sum of the engagement with an organization, not the individual parts.

To build the AES that's right for your business you need to take metrics from across the groupings in the consolidated funnel, not weighting too much toward the top, middle or bottom, making sure that these are the metrics that relate best to how you engage with your customers. For example, a sales representative working on closing a deal for product A sees that the AES for that company is very high and views the data driving this high score, seeing that there have been website visits and video views from the staff at his target account on issues relating to product X. With this information she references the benefits of product X as a follow-on purchase to product A for which she has already built the customer engagement, also, hopefully, increasing the positive perception of her within the target account as she is looking to help with another of their business challenges.

Intent analysis gives you a view outside of the raw numbers by account of what the organization are looking into. Set up correctly, this can give you actionable insight that allows you to interact more successfully with your target accounts. There are many organizations that can provide third-party intent data, which takes web traffic information from many sources and maps it to domain names. This can be added to your own first-party intent data based on an account engagement score also by key topic areas to provide a full intent summary that can be used to guide your business. The aim here is to focus the business more effectively and allow you to deploy your resources where it makes sense. Historically you may have been in a situation where a whole marketing or sales campaign was run to a potentially lucrative part of the market only to find afterwards via the campaign that the opportunity was not as hoped; maybe a competitor had beaten you to it, or an unknown niche regulation meant it wasn't viable, or any number of issues. The use of intent data aims to help reduce this issue by understanding the target businesses that are engaging around certain topics that your organization can address.

The outcome here is for the business to move to be proactive in engagement, not reactive. The opportunity that this represents is huge and is at the heart of Smarketing.

The challenge of measurement, reporting and governance

The reality is that to achieve what is outlined above is no mean feat. The challenge of getting to a single report for the whole customer engagement cycle and the corresponding account engagement score isn't straightforward. As you have read this you have no doubt thought of the many and varied blocks to achieving these two objectives within your organization, and here we outline some of the main ones and the ways to overcome them.

Challenge 1

The first challenge is the ever-apparent people challenge of unifying the two departments; this will often be the biggest stumbling block. As with any change management project, bringing the people along the journey is central to success and this is no different. We outlined in Chapter 5 a number of the challenges in general about people and these all apply to the operations teams as well. Broadly, though, with the appointment of a single leader and the immediate adoption of specific projects in the move to Smarketing the teams will start to evolve and change. Unlike some of the actual execution teams within the Smarketing department, the skills of the operations teams will often be similar, just applied to different parts of the business. This will also help in expanding the scope of a role rather than more fundamental change.

Challenge 2

Following on from this, the systems the business uses are going to be a major factor in achieving Smarketing and the CRM system sits at the core of this. Overall the CRM processes and set-up should not be changed too much; it's more about the virility of the data and the enablement of the teams using the CRM, as covered in Chapter 9. The key is to enable the reporting and data held by the CRM system, harnessing it via the operations team to give the evolved Smarketing view we advocate.

Alongside the CRM system, web analytics and roles to understand online interaction with your organization are also vital. This is the historical domain of marketing and the area where a lot of focus is needed to help add this data in a meaningful way to build out the first-party intent view via the account engagement scoring. The use of the latest web analytics tools and specifically domain tracking will help to successfully provide the insight needed. Even if it is not possible to deliver any domain tracking (and there are many reasons that this might be the case) then look to use more traditional methods to understand the company or account your visitors are from. It might be that the implementation of a simple form asking just that question provides the solution. For example, a form on the front of the website saying that 'to help you better please tell us your company name'; then all activity afterwards is aligned to that account even if visitors do interact fully and fill out a complete response or registration form.

Taking these challenges on will help, but the process of delivering a single view that everyone agrees on can still be hard to achieve. There may still be siloed reporting happening within the business where the publishing of these reports might take resources or be at odds with the single view that the operations team are looking to build. There may be use of different terminology, or the adoption of the centrally agreed terms might not be happening at the speed that is needed. Again, it is vital for the operations team to retain focus team in light of these issues; often over time these reporting issues will dwindle as the value of the single centrally produced reporting view is seen. Also, in building the reports they will probably not find the answer to every reporting question, so additional dimensions can be added over time which will help buy-in and reduce separate reporting.

This is an important factor, especially for large, complex businesses where the reporting needs to cover a huge number of different departments within the wider Smarketing team. In many organizations different departments may claim to need different reports due to their business being different. An example of this might be in sales pipeline coverage where one team has a market-leading product or service needing low pipe cover and another team with an old or challenging solution or service might need much higher pipe coverage. These are the sorts of things that the operations team delivering this reporting will have to deal with and should be manageable or form part of a managed process to get the right reporting. In this example, even if this pipeline coverage differs and is not consistent, at the very least the metrics that used to differ should now be the same, so the same data fields, the same product value, consistent or equivalent weighting. Not using differing data fields is really the key here.

People-powered reporting, measurement and governance

To deliver combined Smarketing operations it is clear that strong leadership is needed to drive the change to the Smarketing operations team, and the selection of that individual is central to this. When looking at this as a business it may be that there is clearly a suitable individual or that external hiring is needed, but as the first main step of Smarketing, finding the leader needs focus. When looking at the traits of this person compare them to the Smarketing leader traits to give a view of their core. Alongside this leader there also needs to be strong focus on the team that supports them and it's vital to retain the personnel from the historical separated sales and marketing operations teams. The knowledge that they have built up and their insight into the systems are going to be fundamental to delivering the unification of Smarketing operations. Close partnership with both the Smarketing leader and the HR team should be followed to reduce any loss of staff that a big change project can bring. Being the first team that the Smarketing leader focuses on, with specific meetings, presentations and one-to-ones, will help to reduce this and highlight their importance on the journey to creating the new Smarketing department.

Conclusion

Even if you do nothing else you must fix reporting to give single reports that cover the whole customer engagement cycle. This is the one key thing that underpins Smarketing and as a result, if you achieve this you are well on the way to Smarketing. Over time the departments will evolve and change working based on following the conclusions and insight delivered by the single Smarketing reporting.

Moving from siloed sales and marketing reporting is not an option, it is a requirement of surviving and driving a healthy business in the digital world. A business trying to operate without a view across sales and marketing is in the long term an opportunity for your organization to take market share and once you deliver Smarketing you will see that happening. The importance of the reporting to underpin this in our digital world has never been more relevant, with the pace of change but also the pace of information, and our aim here has been to outline how you can change your operations focus in order to give a better view of your customers, prospects and suspects.

Changing the business from being reactively driven by backward-looking analysis of the things that have already happened, to one that looks forward using intent data will come from changing the approach to operations and the reporting that this vital team delivers. Over time the use of these reports will evolve and the aim should be that this also moves outside of Smarketing to give the whole organization insight into the reporting and the conclusions that are drawn from reports. This is where the operations team can empower the

Smarketing leader and help them to take the organization forward proactively.

For the people involved this should be a hugely exciting transition that is seen in a very positive light as an effort to help the business thrive, with operations at the heart of it. For any operations professional with the right attitude, the opportunity that this represents will be what drives them to deliver the best for Smarketing.

Questions to ask yourself

1 Are you reliant on other people's departments to write the reports needed or will you be able to justify your own PMO (project management office)?

2 Is your CRM system still fit for purpose? Assuming it is, do you have the relevant reports to support this programme covering sales, marketing and operations? If not then do you need to gather user requirements?

3 While the Smarketing programme should not impact on the forecast process, people may apportion blame for any dip in the forecast that occurs, maybe from outside circumstances, changes in process or just from working on better data. Are you aligned to support this in terms of process and politics?

4 The last thing you need is figures not agreeing; have you created time in the project for testing and making sure figures in different systems reconcile?

5 If sales and marketing are going to share the forecast, are people aligned and ready to understand where different teams have responsibility? For example, you wouldn't expect sales to manage everything from an MQL/MQA. People also need to understand that certain ratios, for example win/loss, don't need to be measured from the top of the funnel.

Practical tools to support your Smarketing programme

09

Technology is nothing. What's important is that you have a faith in people, that they're basically good and smart, and if you give them tools, they'll do wonderful things with them.
STEVE JOBS

Introduction

In this chapter we will talk about different types of data, first and third party, and some of the tools you might use. Previously we have mentioned intent data; in this chapter we will look at how data can be used to help us make informed decisions in our new Smarketing organization.

In the Smarketing world we need to look at measurement of the whole funnel so that stakeholders can understand flow as well as bottlenecks. Previously we have talked about how we need to bring the HR department into the project for aligning compensation as well as people's objectives. We also looked at who can help with the project, and will talk about sales enablement as a function to help 'fix the engine, as you fly the aircraft'.

But when and how do we start?

While this chapter is about tools, it is also about data and business process.

Prussian General Carl von Clausewitz, Vom Kriege said, 'The enemy of a good plan is the dream of a perfect plan.'

There is a cartoon we often use at the end of our training course that has two people about to plant a field. The first person starts to think about fences, what types of fences, should there be a path, how will they water the field. The second person just plants the field. After time the first person (still making decisions about how it will be) looks over at the second person, who is already reaping what they have sown. The moral of the tale is to sometimes just get on with it; you can spend too much time thinking and planning, while actually just doing might be the best approach. I like the inspiring wisdom found in this old Chinese proverb: 'The best time to plant a tree was 20 years ago. The second-best time is now.'

Does the phone ring more?

Adam often says to people when they describe a demand generation initiative, 'does the phone ring more?' This is his metaphor for, does this particular sales or marketing initiative, a banner add, a new logo, telesales, etc make a revenue impact on the business? We won't argue here about the pros and cons of a new logo, but you can argue that unless something makes an impact to the bottom line, as in revenue, why are you doing it?

Hugo also tells the story of how in his role, everybody complained about the poor SEO of his website. They therefore ran a project to brainstorm all the key words and fine-tuned the website, the content as well as running an expensive Google adwords campaign so if anybody searched for those key words, they would scoop them up and turn them into leads. The problem was it created too many leads; they couldn't cope, and when they qualified the leads, they were the wrong type of lead. For example, Hugo's company sold to organizations above a particular threshold and they were inundated with people below that threshold.

A fool with a tool

Grady Booch famously said, 'A fool with a tool is still a fool', so while we will mention a few tools that will help you, we don't want to overwhelm you or come across as biased to one supplier. I recently read a book that used salesforce.com as an example all the way through the book, to the point I assumed it was an advertisement for the company and I just skipped all those pages.

While writing this book we tried to find who said, 'data is the new oil', and it seems to have been said by many people as well as myself. While we can debate this, YOUR data is the most valuable asset you have and will help you in your Smarketing programme: look after it and nurture it.

Let's look at some of the terminology. There are two terms we will use here:

1 **First-party data**: this is the data that you own. What's in your CRM, your marketing automation system, what's in your website, this all belongs to you and you need to treat it like a new car.

2 **Third-party data**: this is data that resides with somebody else. This is not lesser data, in fact it might help you and may actually be cleaner than the first-party data.

Take LinkedIn: this is first-party data and the people on LinkedIn (usually) will have updated it when they change jobs, etc. Whereas the names and job titles in your CRM will have a shelf life, so may not be that up to date.

The chasm between sales and marketing

In the book so far we have talked about the chasm between sales and marketing. Where does marketing finish and sales start? I've had many a conversation about sales being 'execution' of a SQL or SQM, but in the new world of Smarketing we don't have that luxury; the world of commerce moves too fast. One of the areas that needs to be looked at is around objectives and compensation. As compensation drives behaviour the two are intertwined.

Our recommendation is that this now-combined department of sales and marketing (both teams) must have the same interdependent organizational goals. For example, the marketing pipeline should be tied to sales quotas. As part of the common language we discussed before, the teams should have visibility of each other's goals. Probably the most controversial subject is that compensation should be based on shared marketing and sales goals. I'm not saying that some of the more 'fluffy' marketing tactics, such as branding, be abandoned. But the Smarketing organization needs to understand how and what this will achieve for the greater good.

It may be that to start the project, sales and marketing need a service-level agreement between the two departments. Just the process of defining the inputs and outputs, and having a common language would be useful.

Sales enablement

One of the issues that companies have to grapple with as they move to a Smarketing environment is 'how do you change the engine of the aeroplane and continue to fly?' Life goes on. Targets and revenue have to be made. You cannot suddenly stop the company and build the processes and internal culture. You can make changes each new financial year or each half-year, but this still requires time and effort in terms of communicating and educating people internally.

Tim talks about it in his book on social selling, this realization that there needs to be somebody embedded within the Smarketing function that the team trusts and who can work on the further development and evolution of the team.

We think that the term 'sales enablement', which is something that has become popular as a term, is along the right lines. Of course the fact that it's called sales makes people think it is a sales function: it should probably be called Smarketing enablement.

More details on the sales enablement society can be found here: https://www.sesociety.org/home.

Suite vs kit

Suppliers often talk about their product offerings being a suite of applications. In many cases this is a number of applications that cover a business flow, whereas a kit is where the application does a discrete job or function in isolation. We are not aware of a company that has a Smarketing suite of products (a suggested new market maybe); they may do parts, but certainly not the whole flow as we would see it.

Bringing HR into the project

Any change in compensation is going to require a change of people's terms and conditions, which is always a sensitive area. Any Smarketing project, as mentioned previously, isn't just about sales and marketing but has touchpoints with all aspects of the company. The people part of the programme must include HR. Apart from the usual ramifications of compensation you also need to look at:

1 Communication

There has to be a clear communication plan that covers, sales, marketing (of course) but also operations, service, support as well as manufacturing, procurement and supply chain. Let's not forget that manufacturing and supply chain have to forecast what a company is going to sell so they can make the right goods and ship them to be in the right place for the customer. As we talked about earlier when we discussed customer journey mapping, this needs to bring people from as wide a cross-section of the company as you can so you can get feedback and opinions as to customer journeys. These people also can be ambassadors for the company's Smarketing journey to spread the message of the change programme. While often companies stifle debate, in fact you should welcome it; there are people that have worked for you in different departments, maybe with particular skills in certain markets, and they may come up with ideas you hadn't thought about. Of course, many of these people are cynics who have seen many a reorganization. But people will often say, 'I bet they haven't thought of this or that', and that insight is invaluable and worth listening to.

2 Build our staff to have a broader understanding of the funnel

Everybody is a salesperson, and right across the business (aligned with your journey-mapping exercise) this gives you an opportunity to take everybody along on the journey. For example, once the journey map is created you can ask staff to take a look and give their opinions. Publish the map where everybody can see it; this will create a debate. Like a suggestion scheme, people should be encouraged and supported to partake. This debate will also create an education for people who might not know how sales and marketing work in an organization; the warehouse worker for example. Tim's grandfather, J. Donald Hughes, used to run a suggestion scheme for the British Thomson-Houston Company. One of the posters that he designed focused on the simplicity of the spring washer. Regarded as an important detail in the construction of countless electrical and mechanical apparatus, the spring washer is an example of a simple and successful idea that may come from outside of the Smarketing team.

3 Realignment of your team outside of traditional roles

It's not for us to tell you how to organize your employees in the new world of Smarketing, but you might want to look at different roles from those traditionally used in sales and marketing teams. It may be that you try different people for different stages of the funnel. You may argue this is similar to what we have already: Top of the Funnel (ToFu) is marketing and Bottom of the Funnel (BoFu) is sales. To try and bridge the sales and marketing chasm, why not look at a ToFu person, a BoFu person and a 'Middle of the Funnel' (MoFu) person.

4 Human resources (HR)

Apart from the change already required in terms of role responsibilities, compensation and targets, HR will also need to have the new Smarketing leader. As discussed before this is going to be a merger of the traditional sales and marketing leads.

5 Training and enablement

HR will also need to provide the training and enablement required for the changes to roles and responsibilities. A mistake that people make is budgeting for the system change but not for people training and enablement. Or people assume that change can happen either with a one-hour webinar or something delivered over the web. This requires change in people's working practices and it does not happen this way. We recommend the 70:20:10 learning methodology.

70:20:10 learning

The 70:20:10 model of learning is more than just a training fad, it can help predict better organizational success, according to research that suggests it is the most effective learning model and supports the change of working practices. The issue is that during webinars people often do other things like eating their lunch, e-mailing or reading the newspaper. Webinars are fine for disseminating technical information, but not for change.

A study by business transformation consultancy Towards Maturity, '70+20+10=100: The Evidence Behind the Numbers' (Overton, 2016), found that learners who keep to the ratio that 70 per cent of knowledge should come on the job, 20 per cent from observing others, and only 10 per cent from formal training classes will be much better equipped. How many training sessions have you turned up to, where the lecturer shows you 200 PowerPoints slides and you go back to your desk and nothing has changed.

The research revealed that staff following this model were four times more likely to demonstrate a faster response to business change (30 per cent vs 7 per cent), were three times more motivated (27 per cent vs 8 per cent) and were twice as likely to report improvements in customer satisfaction scores.

'Towards Maturity' said that better learning outcomes are gained using this model because the ratio acts as a good rule of thumb that then enables a culture of continuous learning to flow. It found that organizations who stick to this methodology will naturally be four times more likely to provide staff with access to job aids, four times more likely to encourage managers to support learning and 11 times more likely to help staff find what they want through content curation.

However, the study also found that many learning and development (L&D) heads remain sceptical of 70:20:10 because it implies formal learning doesn't work and that the model was simply a way to justify cutting training budgets. Survey results also showed that some L&D heads felt the ratio numbers were set in stone. However, 'Towards Maturity' said such negative or restrictive perceptions were 'myths'.

The study also found those who do use the 70:20:10 model are twice as likely to analyse business problems more thoroughly, three times more likely to involve users in the design of their learning, and seven times more likely to use spaced-out learning to aid retention of information.

Departmental service-level agreement (SLA)

A sales and marketing SLA defines what each team commits to accomplishing in order to support the other in reaching a shared objective or goal. The debate around the SLA will crystallize the alignment around the goals. Let's not forget that SLAs go both ways. Marketing to sales = number of quality leads required to hit company goals, and sales to marketing = speed and depth of lead follow-up that makes economic sense.

In the world of social selling we see that lead generation actually sits in sales; salespeople who have been empowered with social will be using their social networks as proactive demand-generation capability, while marketing focuses on corporate brand. It's worth noting that in the world of social selling, the corporate brand is actually that of the salespeople. People buy from people. The buyers are searching on social and they will find salespeople or trusted advisors. The sales process of today in a social selling organization is that sales own demand generation. This breaks away from the classic 'feast and famine' lead generation which marketing ran or that was the result of legacy sales methodologies such as cold calling.

So what tools do you need?

Our view is that you need to be able to measure metrics covering the whole funnel from top to bottom; from the lowest marketing qualified lead (MQL) or marketing qualified account (MQA) to deals turning into contracts and revenue. The reason you need to measure the whole end-to-end funnel flow is that you will need to fine-tune your process; you will also need to provide reports for stakeholders, department heads as well as the users of the systems. You need to look at lead flow, bottlenecks as well as win/loss.

We realize this sounds like a lot of reports and work: it is. But you can only do what you can do, from the smallest sole trader that might use a CRM like Nimble to a large multi-billion-dollar multinational that might use products from Oracle, Salesforce or Microsoft.

Configure price quote (CPQ)

At this point salespeople will throw the book at the wall expecting a pay cut, whilst marketers are celebrating for joy as they expect a pay rise. In fact, while there may be some realignment, pay rates should stay the same: enter CPQ software.

CPQ (configure price quote) software has been around for a number of years. Errors in sales compensation have often been a problem for many companies. Compensation plans can start off being simple but can grow out of hand. All sales needs is a few errors and dual process is created, where sales create their own spreadsheets to check that finance have calculated the compensation correctly. As well as tying salespeople up in non-sales-related activity, the debates on e-mail and with management can cost thousands in management time.

Let's look at what the acronym CPQ stands for: Configure Price Quote.

C is for Configure

We do not live in a one-size-fits-all world. As a famous Burger King commercial used to remind us, we can have things our way. Not only do we want our burgers configured with just the right toppings, we have also grown to expect everything customized to our wants and needs.

We create custom playlists for our music, build our cars on dealer websites to identify which features best fit our desires and budgets, and can even design our own personalized shoes and jeans online. In our consumer purchases, this desire to configure may be driven by 'want', but in our business purchases, configuration is driven by 'need'. It's a configure-to-order world.

If you are a B2B seller, you must address this need with unique combinations of products and services that deliver exactly what your buyers need. And if you can't do that, then your competition will. CPQ software can enable your sales team to configure your offerings, following your business rules and meeting your customers' needs. In a B2B world, the bill of materials (BoM) of any bid can be complex, with different configurations and options. Each of these lines will have a cost to the client and a relative margin to the supplier, which will be made up of fixed costs, including wages and commission. Different products may have different line items for commission, making it a nightmare for finance departments and payroll to work out.

P is for Price

Few businesses sell their products at full list price to all customers in all situations. Perhaps you offer special pricing, bundle pricing or volume pricing. And maybe your sales reps like to apply extra discounts to 'sweeten the deal'. Keeping track of current pricing, discount rules and bundle pricing can be a headache.

But more importantly, it can be disastrous to the bottom line when discounts are applied incorrectly or inconsistently. And it can be embarrassing when you misquote prices to a customer; it can even cause you to lose the deal. It is common for special deals and/or discounts to only apply to certain products or services. How many times have you walked into a shop where there is a sale and found yourself looking at the rack for this season, which isn't in the sale?

CPQ software helps manage pricing for all your products and services. It enables your sales team to create quotes with consistent pricing, including available discounts, quickly and accurately.

Advanced pricing rules can be set to handle volume discounts, percent-of-total subscriptions, pre-negotiated contract pricing and channel and partner pricing. Using CPQ software you can be sure that your pricing is accurate and optimized.

Q is for Quote

You can't close a deal until you present a quote or proposal. Sales reps spend a lot of time and effort to earn the opportunity to present a quote to a customer, so they need to create the quote correctly and quickly. And it needs to represent the business in a carefully crafted, professional manner. Once again, CPQ software provides the solution.

With just a few clicks, a sales representative (rep) can create a quote, send it in an e-mail, and even include an e-signature to close the deal. CPQ software automatically pulls in the configured products and pricing, tying the whole process together and ensuring consistency.

CPQ software is also the mechanism that allows for approvals to be sorted on quotes, BoM and on levels of discount. It can be used to be routed around a company if there needs to be a hierarchy of approvals. I realize that this sounds like a big company problem, but even in small companies you need to make sure what your salespeople are proposing is profitable for the company.

All of the usual suppliers have them, as well as specialist products. The important point is not the software, but the thinking behind the compensation plans you decide to build behind the software. Critical is the need to align the compensation down the funnel.

Intent data

Typically people see the funnel: note I'm not calling it the sales funnel, because that makes it sound like it belongs to sales. It doesn't, and hopefully we have helped you to understand in previous chapters that it now belongs to everybody, in your new Smarketing function.

In terms of what you might be doing as branding or activity on social media, this is now part of the customer journey, the customer experience (cx). In the world of the internet there may be people out there wanting to buy your products and services and they might not even know you exist.

So what is intent?

If somebody in the process of looking for a product or service starts a search on Google, this could be classed as intent. Looking at a website, this is intent. Watching YouTube videos, reading blogs or white papers or even asking questions like 'I'm in the market for a new car and I wonder what people can recommend?', 'We are think-ing about changing our website, any hints or tips?', 'Our existing accounting system is creaking at the seams, any suggestions?' are all examples of intent and this needs to be listened for.

Brandwatch

Brandwatch is something that we use internally and can be used to listen for topics and what people are talking about. Generally we use it for measuring our clients' social media that we run for them, but it can be used to listen and profile certain personas and definitions of people.

Microsoft Dynamics 365

Microsoft Dynamics 365 Social Engagement helps sales teams discover insights from social posts and identify follow-up actions. For example, 'Can anybody help me with my trash collection?'

With Microsoft Dynamics 365 you can set up 'intent tags' that use machine learning to highlight posts when buying signals or requests for information are identified. We know that sounds a bit like the Starship Enterprise, but actually it is pretty simple to set up.

What we mean by 'machine learning' is the fact it will go away and find 'intent' and give you a list of the top 10, which you can then go through and accept or reject. Each time you accept or reject the machine learns. Obviously, the more you accept and reject the more the algorithm should focus on your requirements. Each sales user can have personalized feeds based on country, sector, vertical, requirement and review posts that match these intent triggers. Once these have been accepted they create new lead records (MQM) in Dynamics 365. This means that sales are empowered to have a fully bespoke listening capability for their territory, rather than something that is aggregated. Dynamics 365 Social Selling Assistant also uses these machine-learning capabilities to give sales users a personalized feed of post recommendations of insight and knowledge to share in their networks, either to take to their next meeting with customers or to share and nurture the network on LinkedIn, Twitter, etc.

Reviewing this list for a few minutes each day enables sales users to discover and share posts that are of interest. The Social Selling Assistant monitors the social accounts and topics that matter to you to help individuals increase their social presence and earn trust by sharing content and participating in conversations.

Bombora: https://bombora.com

Some companies are getting intent information from third-party companies; such a company we are aware of is Bombora. Typical use cases are:

1 Passing intent data to sales, based on certain accounts. This allows salespeople to prioritize and focus on certain accounts. Often people don't even know that evaluations and searches are taking place in accounts they might look after. It also works with existing accounts to guide conversations they might want to have. With any sales approach to a company, if you know little about the account, how do you decide what products or services to mention? Maybe if the intent data from Bombora shows the account is undertaking a lot of searches on machine learning, then that could be your topic of discussion with them?

2 It is also being used by field marketing to prioritize, say, events, by country, locality and vertical. If there is certain intent by life sciences companies in Chicago then maybe you should run an

event there? So just by looking at the intent data that Bombora suggests you can look at topics by area or even events by account.

3 Finally, it can be used to help with deciding where you are going to place advertising, but based on previous chapters, you may find that the power of adverting is dwindling.

We understand that Bombora can be used with Salesforce and other CRM systems, as well as offering the data in e-mail format.

6sense: https://6sense.com/

This product is another that looks for intent and helps companies find accounts that are in active buying cycles for their products and services. It is often used in three different ways:

1 for account-based marketing (ABM) advertising: it allows you to target adverts (if you still think people read them) directionally at those accounts;

2 you can get lists of target accounts of companies that might be searching for the products and services that you sell;

3 where there are searches, you might want to engage early so that you are in the driving seat in the sale, ahead of your competition.

Data management platform (DMP)

I'm aware of one company that ran a campaign to get people to download a white paper. That would usually be a gated piece of content that you can unlock with an e-mail address, that address then being used to continually send you different e-mails to try and market to you. This white paper that marketing drove people to was free to download. The reason for this was that the organization didn't want the customer's e-mail address, they wanted the prospect's cookie. In fact the cookie is the modern battleground.

Most of us would admit that we use different devices at different times of the day. Maybe it's mobile on the way to work, PC at work, mobile on the way home again and Apple Mac at home. Either way this means you are completing different searches and cookies from those searches will be placed on those different devices. You can segment your audience by device and audience. For example, you might want to target a person's mobile on a Saturday as they might have their guard lowered and be more accepting of your message. This can make your advertising more targeted and also help you look at retargeting to better manage your adverting dollars. This does all assume that you believe that advertising and being a brand that 'broadcasts' and 'interrupts' is a good place to be.

Expert-to-expert communication

Whilst not wanting to jump ahead with regard to ABM, which we talk more about in Chapter 10, from a tool perspective in the world of enterprise B2B, we do not need to do mass marketing; often we know or can research which customers we need to talk to. We are therefore talking about one-to-one marketing or one-to-few marketing.

The modern buyer is looking for an expert. They have a business issue and they are looking for a person and a solution that can solve it. In the realms of expert speaking to expert there is a tool called Passle.

Getting experts to 'talk' online is often difficult; people are reluctant to blog and Passle can be the solution. We have all read an article and had a 'feeling' welling up inside that we could put down on paper. Passle allows you to do this. You highlight the area in the article, write your point and feelings down and then you can share on social. A company can also have its own Passle page, which is connected to your website and allows you to get the usual search engine optimization (SEO) and 'Google juice' benefits.

There is also a feature called ISATOY – I Saw and Thought of You. This allows you to find a piece of content and send it directly to a prospect, contact or customer: in other words a one-to-one, totally focused communication. This is an excellent relationship builder in a social selling and ABM world.

Demand generation ready-built process and software

There is also the Sirius Decisions (https://www.siriusdecisions.com) set of tools, software and methodologies. We haven't used it so can't express an opinion, but we know that it has been used and it might be an option to evaluate.

Analysis/paralysis

The next section looks at a high level at reporting, which we have covered in a previous chapter around the people and the process. As a short warning, you also need to think about not creating so many reports that you make no decisions; have clear objectives and measure those. There may be day-to-day reports you look at, but don't lose sight of the overall objectives, and one of those as a company is to make money and do right by your customers.

Closed-loop reporting

In simplistic terms this makes sure that everybody gets to understand what is going wrong or right and, if it does go wrong, the way that this is fed back. In the past, marketing fed sales with leads. Sales complained that the leads were rubbish. At no time did sales explain why the leads were rubbish and so nothing changed. Marketing's reference points stayed the same and they kept sending the same type of leads.

This allows your team to get up-to-date account and contact data; you can learn which programmes are working and which are not. This should increase your ROI (return on investment).

More so, closed-loop reporting should analyse marketing sources (organic, social, referral, etc) where you are getting the most customers and the most revenue. This conversation data will allow you to understand which content is creating the most customers and revenue, and provide a timeline of interactions with contact prior to them becoming a customer. This allows you to understand what in the marketing mix needs to be 'dialled up' or 'dialled down'.

In a joined-up Smarketing world you should also be able to give feedback throughout the sales process. People often think that 57 per cent of the process takes place online, and the rest is then one-to-one with a salesperson: this is not the case. As we mentioned earlier, in fact while a customer is in dialogue with a salesperson they may well also be searching for things online, backing up decisions or undertaking further research. The ability to automatically send your sales team alerts when prospective customers revisit the website or take key actions and to provide a mechanism for when best to make contact is critical as part of your application plan for Smarketing.

What are the typical reports you will need?

Some typical dashboards you might like to implement as part of your Smarketing programme are:

- Measure and communicate progress towards primary goals as agreed in the SLA.
- Measure volume of leads or volume of quality leads against the monthly goal and check daily.
- Track leads by source – set goals by source and measure progress.
- Track leads by campaign – which efforts successfully drive traffic, leads and customers?
- Track the volume of MQLs, which types are generated.
- Monthly marketing report – do a full analysis on monthly basis to dig into important metrics and evaluate why you did or did not hit the targets. Share across the company. The mistake people often make is to share reports with no content, even in a beautiful format. People need insight for success and failure and often this is more important than the report itself.
- Sales by day dashboard – measure progress towards the sales goal and compare with last month.
- Sales activity reports – for example, leads worked by month.

It is important to share a common dashboard with reports aligned to team goals. If we think about British football (soccer), each team is different and some teams are better than others; that is why it is divided into leagues. In your dashboards, don't put a Premier League team against a League Two team; it is not motivational for either team. Align teams that are alike. For example, we got one company that is a client of ours to split away 'business development' and so separate non-quota-carrying salespeople from quota-carrying sales-people. Check the dashboard daily and encourage teams to fix problems.

What to do when things go wrong

It's far too easy to rely on the behaviours of the past and start 'throwing stones at people' across e-mail. You must rely on data, not emotions. You have to separate reality from perception. The 'salespeople are lazy' and the 'leads are poor' excuses have to stop; with Smarketing you are all in it together. Finger pointing does not solve problems; collaboration does.

How do we maintain open communication?

Weekly Smarketing meeting. There needs to be a weekly Smarketing meeting where your entire sales and marketing teams attend to get on the same page, talk about team successes, product information, personal education and SLA waterfalls.

Monthly management meeting. This meeting is held with the stakeholders to discuss topics in depth and act as an escalation point for any issues. As we have talked about earlier in terms of the new leadership required for Smarketing, people need to feel that this isn't a sales-driven meeting and it's not a marketing-driven meeting. If people think decisions are pre-judged, then they won't escalate.

Conclusion

In this chapter we have taken you through a tour of some of the tools you will need in this new Smarketing world. Smarketing will need you to look at compensation, always an emotive issue, and some of the tools that can help streamline it. We have also looked at the need to move our organizations away from reactive lead forms to proactive intent data. Finally we have looked at some of the reports you might need. With reporting, every company is different, but we have tried to give you a starter kit to enable you to start your thinking and debate internally.

Questions to ask yourself

1 Are you able to measure the amount of inbound you are getting? Can you measure the number of (additional) leads and meetings you are acquiring through Smarketing? (We asked earlier if your CRM was still fit for purpose.)

2 Have you thought about adequate training for employees on any new tool you may deploy? Training should cover people, process and the new tool.

3 If you don't have sales enablement (Smarketing enablement) is it time to invest in a person, a team or teams of people who can support your marketing and sales team in this process shift?

4 With the process change you are thinking about, will you make an investment in any new software? If so, what?

5 Which meetings will people from the old world of sales and marketing be involved in? Obviously, not everybody can still go to each other's meetings, but maybe you want representatives in attendance?

References

Overton, L (2016) In-Focus: 70+20+10=100: The evidence behind the numbers, *Towards Maturity*. Available at: https://towardsmaturity. org/2016/02/02/in-focus-702010100-evidence-behind-numbers [Last accessed 25 May 2018]

Sales Enablement Society (2018) Available at: https://www.sesociety.org/ home [Last accessed 25 May 2018]

Account-based marketing – a new way to organize sales

10

Account-based marketing is a strategic approach that coordinates personalized marketing and sales efforts to open doors and deepen engagement at specific accounts.
JON MILLER, CEO AND CO-FOUNDER, ENGAGIO

The previous chapters have taken you through why you should move to Smarketing, as well as providing a process to enable you to make that move. We have also taken you through how you should measure, what will go wrong and how you should manage it. In this chapter we will take you through a new go-to-market for the brave new world of the connected economy and the educated buyer, where sales and marketing work together in one organization.

The internet-empowered, social-savvy buyer does not buy alone, they hunt in packs. Sales and marketing can no longer sell to one friendly contact; they need to position themselves across the organization, talking to the information technology (IT) as well as business and user departments.

The more leads the better?

'Leads' still seem to be created by buying lists and spraying out e-mails, PPC (pay-per-click), Facebook Ads, or buying your way up Google search. This, you hope, will make an individual in an organization aware of you. The theory is, if you 'touch' a person (currently you are supposed to do this six times) then this person will be interested in your product. Or of course you will have annoyed them so much you will have switched them totally off your brand.

Rhiannon Prothero – Marketing Director UK & Ireland, SAP

… if you think about the journey over time, the end point is someone that has to sit down, have a hard negotiation with somebody, put pen to paper and get it done. Sales want all the credit for that and are welcome to take it.

We measure everything relentlessly to see our impact and one of our key measures is 'pipeline that closes', ie one booked revenue that originated with something that we did and what we get out of that is we're literally high-fiving around the office: 'We found that customer and look what they did with it. They took it from a lead and they turned it into business, they closed it and it's a huge deal and everyone's really excited. But we gave birth to that idea.' That was us in the beginning, but we would never say, 'Look at what we closed'. It's where you see your value in the equation

---

As previously mentioned, an inbound request to a company is often now categorized as a marketing qualified lead (MQL). This is then qualified and if it passes certain criteria is passed to 'sales' to undertake discovery, at which point they should turn it into a sales qualified lead (SQL).

We also mentioned the qualification criteria, Budget, Authority, Need and Timescale (BANT), as qualification method. In the Software as a Service (SaaS) world, I would expect an SQL to have need and authority. Budget and timescale will come later, as part of the sales desire creation process. In many cases this comes at the first meeting, as often sales teams will try to close on the first meeting. This is all great in theory, but according to Forrester, only 0.75 per cent of leads become closed revenue.

The problem is not all leads are created equal. Leads fall out as they move through the stages. As we mentioned before, leads are also seen as a single person in a company, which means we are judging a whole company's propensity to buy based on that individual.

What really happens

To summarize, as mentioned before, taking a worse case example, an intern is asked to ring three companies to get details to look at a new telephone system, but that person won't register on a company's lead scoring system and when your inside salespeople call them they won't pass any level of BANT.

Marketing is focused on acquiring leads, not accounts. This means that sales and marketing (also a revenue-creating team) already start off from the 'get go' working at odds with each other.

The traditional sales funnel is designed for a single customer and isn't optimized for multiple decision makers.

What I want is one lead

This endless drive to create more and more leads will increase quantity and reduce quality. More leads is not the answer; you have to go wider and deeper into accounts. As previously mentioned, most lead-generation campaigns assume a linear path. Looking back to CEB Research, they say that people now self-educate for 57 per cent of the sales process and decide their requirements 37 per cent of the way through. If you are focused on filling your funnel with leads that already have need you may find they don't need you and a competitor has already influenced the buying process.

For example, you may find that a prospect, as part of their self-education, will have defined a requirement you don't provide. If you are 'lucky' enough to get on the shortlist you have to spend all your time 'unpicking' those requirements, rather than focusing on your value proposition. You may have already lost that sale and the argument might be to focus elsewhere. The problem is that you come second in a sale, gobbling up internal resources.

Is there a different path?

In 2006, Seth Godin wrote about flipping the funnel (Godin, 2006). What he meant by that was empowering your fans and community to be talking about you, rather than a corporation talking about itself.

People are more likely to listen to a friend or a family member than a corporate mouthpiece. Enter account-based marketing.

Let us clear something up: while it has the name account-based marketing, let us not think this is a marketing responsibility and hopefully we have convinced you of the need for Smarketing. Therefore, the term account-based everything (ABE) is often applied and is more appropriate. For the rest of this chapter we will carry on with the term account-based marketing (ABM).

ABM is different from traditional sales, which is where you take a list, find my name, call me up or e-mail me then try to force me through a sales pipeline by a push mechanism of continual calls and e-mails, until I buy. With ABM, you don't spend time, effort and budget chasing low-quality leads; you concentrate on a focused lead and build out from there within an account (immediately, since for once marketing and sales are both account-focused and aligned).

ABM requires you to focus on a set of accounts and expand out from your 'bridge head' to include people in different user departments. It's better still if you can 'land and expand', for example, talking to IT, Finance, HR, IT architecture, etc.

To expand and engage contacts in different accounts requires different content. Finance will require different content to IT for example. Utilities companies will require different content than the Telco industry or public sector. Content needs to be personalized and the more personalized the better in terms of business issues and vertical. After all, we all see ourselves as individuals and not 'personas', as many marketers often want to segment us into.

The persona marketing mistake – the perils of segmentation

Businesses often go down the path of personas and segmentation and as we have seen before, this can often lead to confusion in accounts. An example we often used in our training sessions is a persona like this:

Male
Born 1948
Grew up in the UK

Divorced and remarried
Grown-up children
Extremely wealthy
World famous

While this seems like a great narrow focus, it is the same persona for Prince Charles, heir to the throne to the United Kingdom as it is for Ozzy Osbourne, lead singer of the rock band Black Sabbath and a solo artist in his own right. Same persona, very different people, backgrounds and probably different wants and needs.

What ABM enables us to provide

ABM provides organizations with a method to use their digital marketing and social selling skills to educate and engage right up and down the funnel. This engagement will also allow sales and marketing teams to build deep relationships. These relationships mean that seller and marketer should understand an industry's pain points and motivations. As sales and marketing are working together, the organization is able to fine-tune the value proposition and content to focus on the account's business issues as well as the individual's wants and needs.

I've seen ABM initiatives where engagement was seen as sending a newsletter introducing a new salesperson. On the basis that many people don't read cold e-mail, this could be deemed a waste of effort.

Old-school one-to-one relationships

Sales and marketing have always been based on relationships and in the past this has often manifested itself in account reviews. We have undertaken these with salespeople where that person is literally talking to just one person in an account.

If you look at sales methodologies you will hear the terms 'coach', 'angel', or 'inside salesperson'. This is a person who wants your product or service to win, so they help guide you through the organization. In salespeople reviews, this one person they talk to is often presented to sales management as this person who has this role. The danger is that this person is actually spending little or no political capital to help you; they just like talking to you. We recall one sale where the customer was writing a report to go to the board of directors and they spent the weekend talking to the competition. The prospect put us forward as the recommendation on the Monday; they had been talking to the competition to justify them out, not in.

Another way only talking to one person can be dangerous is that you can be bypassed by the competition. We are aware of an existing 'on premise' customer where an SaaS provider bypassed the existing system support team and contacted the finance director (the overall decision maker) direct with a disruptive offer. A decision was made against the existing 'on premise' provider, with no knowledge to the existing support team and supplier.

In addition, having only one relationship in the account places you at risk, not only of being blindsided by the competition, but also losing to the biggest competitor to everybody: doing nothing.

Where should you apply ABM?

You should apply ABM in a Smarketing environment, if you also have any of the following business issues within sales and marketing:

1 you have been asked to grow revenues with no (or little) extra budget;

2 you are seeing cold-calling results fall off a cliff;

3 you find that your inside sales cannot convert inbound;

4 there is competitive pressure;

5 you are in need of a methodology to enable you to sell to an ever more complex set of customers (different buyers, different cultures...);

6 you are working with a client base where you get 80 per cent of the revenue from 20 per cent of the customers;

7 you want to offer a more personalized service to your clients.

ABM can be applied in many forms, not just in 'big accounts' but across the spectrum of from big to small, such as SMEs. It does require you as an organization to focus, which can for some organizations be scary as there can be a level of reassurance in throwing mud at the wall and hoping it will stick. The reassurance is in activity; if we are doing 'something' then that's good, isn't it? Given the choice between 200 leads that create nothing and one lead that converts to revenue, I would take the one lead every time.

What is account-based marketing?

According to Kogan Page's *A Practitioner's Guide to Account-Based Marketing* (Burgess and Munn, 2017) ABM is defined as:

> Treating individual accounts as markets in their own right. Then to position your company and its services with the aim of acquiring a greater share of clients' business and earning continued loyalty...

According to research by Ascend2 in January 2018, the number one reason that people implemented ABM was to align sales and marketing initiatives, followed by attributing marketing efforts to revenue.

In the same report, such a plan was 95 per cent successful, which isn't a bad success rate.

What can be achieved with ABM?

Most organizations look to 'increase share of wallet', that is enable the business to up-sell and cross-sell. It always being easier to sell to existing clients than to new ones.

In the B2B world, companies often have multiple value positions to sell. Certainly in the SaaS world, solutions are sold on the basis of 'land and expand'. This means sales teams sell a pilot or low-value system, often below the radar of IT departments or certain purchasing limits so that a solution is sold which then starts being proven to be a business benefit to that organization. Often this is a small point solution or solving a niche problem. The solution provided is run as a pilot; hopefully it will be a success, at which point you can expand.

Building on the success of the project a supplier can start building relationships with other people and parts of the organization to work on the expansion. This certainly seems to work well, as referencing your own organization as an end user is often seen as an easy option. 'They are already a supplier to us' will save a lot of effort in dealing with procurement or legal.

Change perception or positioning

It may be that you have supplied a solution in the past that is seen as 'old' or forms part of some 'legacy', or maybe you supplied a solution that wasn't deemed as successful as you might have hoped for. Again, many SaaS providers have an ABM policy for salespeople; their job is to take the existing project and grow it. The salespeople are compensated for the growth of ARR (annual recurring revenues), the monthly or quarterly payment companies make for SaaS/Cloud-based solutions.

It might also be that customer service teams are involved in the account as well as sales and marketing in terms of changing a perception. If projects have not gone as well, maybe showing greater level of service is needed to change the perception from negative or neutral to positive.

Develop new accounts

Often ABM is seen as a way of developing existing accounts; in fact ABM can be used to help develop new accounts. This can be done on a one-to-one basis or as a batch if there is a level of similarity such as business requirement and/or vertical market.

For example, we are aware of one company that sold a solution to a wine company; this required them to develop certain functionality about the measurement and transportation of fluids. After that project was successful they approached all wine companies, whiskey distillers, in fact anybody that created liquid products to sell them a solution. Certainly in the wine and whiskey market they became market leaders.

In fact, we are aware of companies that have tried to unseat them, but the intellectual property (IP) created to meet the wine and whiskey producers' requirements, plus the reluctance of companies toward the disruption of changing systems, created a barrier to entry for the competition. You are only going to change systems if there is a clear, compelling reason, and that would require a system to be better. If you are trying to break into a market, that is a large research and development input on the basis somebody 'might' change.

Revenue

We are told from an early age in sales and marketing that it costs more to create a new account than it does to develop an existing account. Therefore, analysis and segmenting your existing accounts and focusing on them must be a priority. Regardless that some of them may not have purchased from you in a long time, people change and requirements change; lowering the bucket into the well has to be a priority.

Long-term relationships

Relationships in accounts are not just about selling and revenue. Building relationships can impact in many ways, creating reference sites to help sell new, other accounts or even land and expand in that account. Which brings us on to referrals.

Referrals

Referrals are a great way to build a network of connections in an account, vertical market or territory. Referral selling is also critical for the salesperson today. Look at your network; is there an account you would like to talk to? Is there somebody in your network that can refer you on? Don't forget that with referrals (as mentioned in the earlier research) you have a higher rate of closure and often in many cases there is little or no competition.

How do you decide which accounts to focus on?

To kick off an ABM project you need to decide which accounts you will focus on. In sales as in marketing it is critical to segment accounts; understanding who not to sell to is just as important, as it's pointless expending energy where you will get no return. One of the ways to understand where to focus is to define your ideal customer criteria.

What are your ideal customer criteria?

Industry, size, turnover, profit? Do you want to focus on big accounts or are you better off selling to SMEs? Some companies focus on a segment in the middle, on the basis that often selling to big companies and small companies takes the same effort. While big companies often have bigger returns and budgets, dealing with them can be time-consuming and can have long sales cycles. Small companies, especially owner-managed companies, can be time-consuming as the owners treat the company money as their money. Sometimes a happy medium is needed.

Contacts

In the world of social media your network is power. When we started our new company in September 2016, the first people we talked to were our network. Your network is where you have a collection of people with probably similar interests that you can call up and go and meet them. All of these people know you and will take your call. It's important to say that it might not be your contact that you are selling to; you may actually be looking for a referral to somebody else within your contact's organization or even somebody else in their network.

Selling to your network as a salesperson or marketer is critical. Big or small, using your employees' networks to sell and market as well as selling through their networks is a critical and fairly simple way to approach new and existing accounts.

Current 'share of wallet'

'Share of wallet' (SoW) is an Americanism that has been used a lot by IT vendors. It is a marketing term referring to the amount of the customer's total spending that a business captures in the products and services that it offers. Increasing the share of a customer's wallet a company receives is often a cheaper way of boosting revenue than increasing market share. Working with clients to grow SoW from 1 per cent to 2 per cent of a company's IT spend, while it does not seem a lot, could, for a big company be millions, and of course you have the satisfaction that you are taking money from competitors.

Development potential

Earlier we used an example of a company that won a contract then targeted similar companies to make more sales. This will often be required to recoup the cost of development, but also to generate revenue. It may be that you want to target accounts on the basis that you want to take the company in a particular development direction.

For example, we are aware of a company that wanted to develop employee advocacy software, so targeted companies on a joint development basis. Not every company will want an untried and tested system, but many will often want to get in at a ground level as they know that they will get greater attention from the vendor and often a system closely 'bespoke' to their needs.

Your market position

Are you a market leader or a start-up? Often companies that you are selling/marketing to will have a risk profile and you need to understand this. Not everybody will work with a start-up; there again, often companies don't like working with market leaders.

Can you work together?

Critical today is cultural fit. The supermarket Walmart in the United States has 'meet and greet,' who are people that stand at the entrance of the supermarket, engaging with customers as they arrive, being the friendly face. Americans like being greeted by somebody with a smile, or maybe they are in a hurry and just want that person to point out where the bread is. Walmart's first expansion outside the United States was via a 'cookie cutter' approach, an approach which believed that what was good for the United States would be good for everywhere else. In Germany, Walmart didn't fit culturally and they actually withdrew from the market. Germans don't like being met by a 'meet and greeter' and just didn't shop there. Cultural fit is important, especially if you are selling to different countries and cultures.

Does your customer have an innovation culture?

Companies have different cultures. For example, the public sector (federal sector in the United States) has a different attitude to risk and innovation than, say, the private sector. If we take the US software company Oracle, a company we have all worked at in the past, while being a large company that can often be conservative in decision making, it prides itself on having a culture that can turn 'on a dime'. The CEO, Larry Ellison, would decide to reorganize the company overnight and the 100,000 employees would fall in line. For example, he decided the company would be an SaaS/Cloud company, literally overnight, and all strategy, go-to-markets etc had to be changed.

Some organizations would have just metaphorically folded their arms and said no, and even worked to stop changes from being implemented. At Oracle you understood change was probably the one factor that didn't change in today's world. Selling to companies that will change or won't change must be a factor in choosing which accounts you target with ABM.

ABM implementation model

The objective of this chapter is to give you an overview of ABM and cite examples to motivate you to implement your own programme as part of the Smarketing programme. As part of any implementation, we always recommend that you start small, prove it and then build it out. Let's start with the pilot.

ABM pilot

In the pilot you will:

- **Determine the pilot accounts**: Start with a handful, don't try to boil the ocean.

- **Develop metrics**: It's imperative you measure from where you started to see if there is any movement.

- **Research and analyse pilot accounts**: It's worth spending time on this. Don't work on 'gut'; you need to make sure that the accounts meet your strategy requirements as well as the criteria above.

- **Build an integrated account plan and execute**: The mistake that people often make is that sales and marketing work in silos and they both create different account plans. There needs to be one plan created jointly.

- **Measure and review:** It's critical that you measure regularly with the relevant stakeholders; this allows you to make changes if you are not getting the right results. Or at least have buy-in and visibility of the programme.

- As we discussed earlier in terms of communications methods, you must publicize the results. With any change programme you need to have a communication plan; sharing with people your successes and failures is important as success breeds success and admission of failures shows honesty. People like success and honesty and are more likely to support your programme either in this pilot stage or when it comes to rolling it out.

Build stage

The next stage is the 'Build' phase where, as it says, you will 'build' on the pilot. ABM does require a change in attitude and working practice, which will require people, as with any change programme, to work differently. The Build process could be called the Pilot Plus stage; things are not yet 'business as usual', in fact you are probably still experimenting with what works and what does not. Admission of failure is key to stop wasted time and effort. But you are also creating your own company plan and understanding of what for you is best practice.

In this stage you need to gather learnings from the pilots, which may include refining the account selection. A classic mistake is that people start nominating accounts for the programme, not based on the programme success criteria, but on thinking it would be good for their customer. Like a 'gold' account programme, all salespeople want their customers to think they are gold customers.

You also need to make sure you define common metrics and success criteria. This may or not be revenue; if you are changing perceptions or have a customer service focus then maybe the measure is a reduction in support calls or more positive results from a customer service questionnaire.

Where will you get the budget? Identifying funding sources is critical. Often within companies, budget does not come out of one 'pot'; you may need source funding from content, digital, sales or alliances budgets. Having such budgets and funding in different places often hampers sales and marketing efforts and maybe how this is organized. The governance going forward is something you need to debate as part of your Smarketing implementation. It's critical that Finance is onside and kept in the loop during such a reorganization so that budgets and cost codes can be maintained. Finally, you must deepen executive sponsorship. Senior-level relationships are critical, not just for buy-in to the project, but for long-term investment.

Standardize

The next phase is to standardize, build it into the everyday working practices and culture, having people thinking ABM from the 'get go', not something they might add to the end of an agenda.

In this phase you need to:

- Create a PMO (programme management office) and governance model. This is about the success of the programme. Stick to the criteria; it isn't about going back to a numbers game. The PMO can look after day-to-day questions as well as creating the monthly reports, freeing up some of the leadership team to focus on the results and success.

- Determine standard metrics and success criteria across all accounts. This is just as much about making sure you get the right accounts in the programme as keeping the wrong accounts out. Having criteria that accounts have to meet means you can prove the wrong accounts are kept at bay. The programme should not be diluted as the success will be diluted. Don't let people bully you into accepting accounts. As we mention above, the salesperson often thinks that all their accounts are 'strategic' and need special treatment.

- Compensation drives behaviour; you need to integrate ABM into the overall award and compensation plan. As part of any ABM and Smarketing programme, sales compensation needs to be reviewed so that everybody is motivated to do right by the customer (first) and your organization (second).

At this point you are ready to scale. Our advice would be to keep the pilot, build and standardize in one country so you are not dealing with country or culture differences. When you do move into different countries, while there is a centralized learning I would plan for local differences. While it's tempting to scale up, our recommendation would be to initiate a pilot phase to make sure you embed cultural differences.

Scale

At the scale phase companies should be achieving economies of scale through standard process, shared services and automation. Often we see 'random acts of ABM' as different departments or countries run their own programmes with no cross-fertilization of ideas. It's all too easy for a team or department to go it alone, but it needs to be coordinated with an organization-wide understanding of strategy, governance and measure.

Understanding stakeholders in an ABM account

Companies often think of accounts in the sales hierarchical structures that are detailed in organization charts. With the power of the internet and social media, it does not work like that anymore. We see a different set of stakeholders within an account or decision-making unit (DMU).

For example, we see the following stakeholders:

- **Buyers:** These are people within the user department that might have a say in the purchase or procurement. Across all products costs are reducing and decision making can take place right down to user level, with a one-use entry-level system.

- **Decision makers:** These people would normally be C-level or main board directors; they probably are able to sign a cheque. Nowadays it is a metaphorical cheque they are signing, but they have direct monetary influence on the buying process.

- **Influencers:** Everybody has influence, from friends people may call upon within a network that might have an influence on a decision, to micro-influencers (bloggers etc), macro-influencers (people such as Daniel Newman @danielnewmanIV or Brain Solis @BrianSolis) and companies like G2, Gartner, Forrester, KPMG, Accenture, Deloitte, etc.

  It's worth noting that people may have influence but no authority; these people are sometimes called changemakers or mobilizers.

- **Initiators:** These are people who will start a project, probably not finishers. As sales and marketers we often have to join up the starters with finishers so that projects started end up being completed.

- **Users:** End users of the system often have influence over what the product looks like (the user experience (UX)) and often make a decision on a product's looks during product demonstration. As I mention above, while users do not have authority, they may have influence. Often I've worked for organizations where there is somebody (sometimes it was me) who a decision maker would ask, 'Is this product any good? Should we go with it?'

Conclusion

We wanted to give you a practical solution to enable your go-to-market as part of a Smarketing programme you initiated. Regardless of whether you are a big or small company, ABM can be implemented and is a great technique to be used in reaction to why people buy today. It provides scale in terms of meeting a company's need to buy in groups. It also provides for both sales and marketing to work to grow networks, create content, and prospect through social, where your clients are.

That brings us to the end of the why and the how of Smarketing, so what about the future? In the final chapter we talk about how we see the world developing.

Questions to ask yourself

1 Would ABM be applicable in your company?

2 Would getting wider and deeper in accounts or using ABM as a way to keep existing accounts be a useful strategy?

3 If you are already using ABM where are you in your implementation cycle?

4 Are you engaged with the right stakeholders across the business?

5 Do you have the right processes in place to make sure ABM doesn't turn into a free-for-all?

References

Ascend2 (2018) Account-based marketing strategy, *Survey summary reports on digital marketing strategies and tactics*. Available at: http://ascend2.com/research/ [Last accessed 25 May 2018]

Burgess, B and Munn, D (2017) *A Practitioner's Guide to Account-Based Marketing*, Kogan Page, London

Godin, S (2006) *Flipping the Funnel* [ebook] Available at: http://sethgodin.typepad.com/seths_blog/2006/01/flipping_the_fu.html [Last accessed 25 May 2018]

Conclusion 11

Over the pages of this book we have built an argument for Smarketing which we hope is strong enough for you to take action and start to implement this in your organization. Let's be honest, the fact that you're even reading this book probably means that you have either been wanting to explore this area or you just realized in a rather *Matrix*-like way, that 'something wasn't quite right' and you couldn't put your finger on it.

The case for change

The case for change is very obvious to anyone working in this area. 'Old' marketing doesn't work; the advent of changing (or changed) customer behaviours powered by the internet and social media has driven a seismic shift in how people buy. Marketing departments the world over have grappled with these changes and their ramifications for their business, but so often this has been a case of evolution rather than revolution. The internet has revolutionized the amount of information that is available to customers, but marketing departments have opted to evolve (as opposed to transform) to meet this change.

The adoption of e-mail marketing is, to marketers, simply an electronic letter, the website, an electronic brochure etc. Even though the technology has changed out of all recognition the thinking behind how that technology should be applied hasn't really changed at all.

Allied to this, sales has not really changed either, although arguably, because they are at 'the sharp end' of the interactions they have been able to get on the change journey early so their behaviour has evolved to stay in step with the customer. However, salespeople are still 'blunt instruments' and they, like everyone else, are resistant to change.

Mind the gap between sales and marketing

You will have seen that customers are often falling between the gap that exists between sales and marketing departments, both in terms of the tactical 'who owns the customer now' at any given point, and from a strategic perspective of understanding what this customer actually wants at each moment.

Rhiannon Prothero – Marketing Director UK & Ireland, SAP

Envision a really basic marketing campaign of some kind where we're doing digital outreach, whatever, and we're managing to capture some responses, right? People are coming to our website, they're looking at whatever it is, the story we've had to tell. Now, somebody has to follow that up in the traditional split of responsibilities; that might be a telemarketer perhaps. They take some live digital input and make a qualifying call.

In reality, though, let's say that's one of our biggest customers. Just because the normal way of doing that would be for a telemarketing follow-up, do we think that's a good customer experience if a sales guy already has a really brilliant relationship with this customer? Do they really want to hear from telemarketing?

It's the most basic of examples, but that's what I'm saying about who does what in any given situation. Because actually, following one of our biggest customers who buys year after year and with whom we are more of a partner than a supplier and we're a key component of their success, I mean it's insulting, right?

If a telemarketer is going to follow me up in that situation I'd be insulted. In fact, I was insulted when I went to buy a car and then two years later someone from their telemarketing team calls. I had multiple negotiations with my one guy. Why is he not phoning me? Suddenly I don't feel very special.

Having a clear vision of what these two departments look like in the future is really important. It is vital to keep your eye on the horizon, that goal for which you as a company are hunting. In order to do that you will need to have a clear vision for what the future looks like, partly so you can retain focus and belief through all of the inevitable ups and downs of the journey, but perhaps more importantly so you can articulate what these departments (or this department) look like to everyone else you will need to take on the journey.

In order though for this vision to be relevant, and not out of date before you even arrive there, you would be minded to consider other changes that are going on in the sales, marketing and technology spaces.

The future of sales and marketing

The reason we advise this is that in 2001, when the internet was in its infancy, very few people considered that the dotcom bubble that had just popped would have little or no effect on the explosive growth of the internet. Many people thought that the web and websites were interesting novelties of the period but rather like the Casio VL Tone pocket keyboard or digital watches, their time was over.

That was profoundly wrong. What we now know for certain is that technological advances are here to stay and that organizations that are able to mount the tech escalator sooner are usually able to harvest a significant advantage over their later-adopting counterparts.

Any look into the future (of which we have a limited view at any given moment) would be most unwise without considering what emerging technologies there are and what they might mean for sales and marketing, for Smarketing, and for business as a whole.

So let's spend a little bit of time thinking about these and the effect that they may have on your plans.

Artificial intelligence

There is a move to use artificial intelligence (AI) in marketing. You cannot seem to move for articles on AI and how it will or won't replace jobs.

When we all started work, there was little adoption of computers in companies. A few people had a Sinclair Z80 or a BBC computer but they were not as mainstream as they are today. In fact, PCs or word processors, as they were called, were not used in businesses.

We had to write all our letters (e-mail was a specialist service used by academics) by hand and they were typed up by a typing pool.

The point is that when the PC was invented it changed working practices and the typing pools disappeared, but these people went on to find other jobs. We don't hear people saying that we should return to those days. AI may well replace some roles but I'm sure those people will be redeployed.

We have been involved in some early AI technology. Nudge (https://nudge.ai/) is an application that takes away the need for salespeople to do research on their accounts and customers. Artesian (http://www.artesian.co/) is something similar.

You may have also used X.ai to book a meeting. X.ai is a personal assistant that uses NLP (natural language programming) so it interacts with you or the person you want to book a meeting with. It works out simple commands like, 'Can we make it next Tuesday?' or 'How about 14:00 on Wednesday 28th', and books the meeting. If you've had a meeting booked with you using it you probably couldn't tell that it was a 'robot' you were talking to. Now we take a step back and move away from the introduction of AI to think about the evolution of mobile phones.

Mobile

During the early days of mobile phones the only thing you could do with them was make calls and send text messages. While text did create a fairly revolutionary step in the way we communicate, there wasn't really anything completely new. The Blackberry just took e-mail (something that had become used by everybody) and turned it from desktop access to mobile access.

With the introduction of the iPhone 11 years ago, people started looking at mobile and thinking differently. Facebook, Snapchat, Twitter; their usage and growth have been driven by this new way of accessing these services. There has also been a growth of new applications and new thinking. Apps such as Shazam (our favourite) and Uber have been built from the ground up, totally new on mobile.

Our point is that AI is still in early stages; it is being used to automate existing processes and technologies and so far nobody really has found new applications (never thought of before) or new ways of working. But that will change, and change probably sooner than later.

AI is already being used as a way to get the right content in front of the right person at the right time. For many this will be a little freaky. You know that feeling, you download a white paper from a website and within five minutes you get a call from a BDR (business development representative) asking you to buy the product or service. For me this happens often; I never have any intention of buying, I just need content to share on social media.

Chatbots

Many brands are experimenting with chatbots. At a recent visit to Pizza Express they had a simple chatbot where you could win something. They were really doing this in a way to collect e-mails to market to later on, but I'm sure there is a team looking to experiment with chatbots at a greater scale. Chatbots are generally being used for customer experience, either pre-sale to answer questions or post-sale to sort problems, such as 'where is my parcel?'

Facial recognition

The iPhone X is one of the first mobile phones to provide facial recognition. This technology is already being experimented with by the social networks as a way of paying for things. That is, you don't use a credit card or money, you use your face to authorize payment.

It cannot be long before our faces become the central item people recognize over and above, say, our e-mail. Regulations in Europe such as GDPR make it so difficult for brands to hold and then market to e-mails that many have simply stopped.

Soon you might use your face as a way to authorize getting offers or discounts. For example, you are walking through an airport, look at an advert or digital kiosk and are sent offers to your mobile or Facebook account. We're not sure if this is creepy or cool but it's not too far away in the future and is something about life I'm sure we will need to get used to.

There was an example of facial recognition used in the 2010 film *Minority Report*, starring Tom Cruise (YouTube, 2010).

The future of AI?

Consumers are digital and mobile. They are craving contact and engagement with other humans and brands and AI in the future will be one of the mechanisms that is more likely to create these interactions.

Most marketing departments are experimenting with AI; it is becoming table stakes and certainly will be in the coming years, so this will, by necessity, form part of your long-term strategy, with or without Smarketing.

How do we visualize the future of social media?

In the film *Bladerunner 2049* there is a future world (no spoilers) inhabited by humans and people who look human, but might not be, there being a morph of humans in to AI, VR (virtual reality) and AR (augmented reality). There are all three.

This is Hollywood's view of the future, but how much is this different from the direction in which social networks are taking us?

Social media today

Think about it, we spend so much time on social media, Facebook, Twitter, LinkedIn, Pinterest they have become like virtual worlds. Facebook is a virtual world of friends and family with maybe a colleague or two. LinkedIn is a virtual world of business, where we can look in on people we don't know, or maybe we do. Pinterest is a virtual world of shopping or projects.

How are VR and AR developing?

If we look at the gaming industry, what they create are virtual worlds, whether it's Angry Birds or World of Witchcraft, and the player becomes immersed in that virtual world. When gaming first started it was single user, you worked in a world against the game; now gaming is multi-user so you are in a world where you work with or against other users. In fact, game makers create an environment where gamers create communities and can battle against each other.

One gamer, who was the world number one at a game, was asked what it was like to be the number one. He said he hated it, as he needed to take five iPads into the shower to stop people burning down what he had created. This shows that for some people virtual worlds are already encroaching on the real world.

Time travel

So how about if I can offer you the ability to travel in time, to a place or time? You could meet and interact with human-like people. Maybe you would want to watch your own birth? Be there when the US Declaration of Independence was signed? In fact, any historical moment. In time, like the gamer above, how would you know if you were in the real world or this new virtual world?

What if you decide you prefer living in 1950s Britain? Is this not what gamers currently strive for? Running home from work to take on their persona in World of Witchcraft for the evening or the weekend? Isn't this what Second Life promised us? In a way, is a Hollywood film an hour and a half of escapism? Or, like the film *Dunkirk*, will take you back to a place in time for two hours?

So the future of social?

We are not friends of Mark Zuckerberg or Jack Dorsey, in fact I'm not sure I know anybody in Silicon Valley (what we are saying is that we are not Silicon Valley insiders) but here is our vision of the future for social.

Let me take a step back here. Social Media has only really been around for about 10 years. There are people that will talk about being in AOL communities and chat rooms before this, which are social. But mainstream social, like we know it today, really came about with the introduction of the iPhone, which is 11 years old. The infrastructure had to be right to allow social to grow and scale.

So our assumption is that we carry on with the infrastructure that we know about right now, mobile phones, VR headsets and AR glasses, but who knows what some clever kid is creating in his or her bedroom somewhere?

So here's our look into the future!

Why can't Facebook, LinkedIn, Pinterest become virtual worlds?

Think about it, why can you not connect with somebody on LinkedIn and meet them in a virtual world? Why should you have to travel right around the world to have that meeting?

Maybe this is what a café company needs to develop. Rather than sitting in a coffee shop, maybe there can be a virtual café, where I can meet and do business with anybody in the world? Or of course, maybe we can do that through LinkedIn.

Tinder could allow you to have a date in a virtual world with anybody in the world. I won't develop that idea further, you can imagine.

One thing we know for certain is that social media is growing at an exponential rate. Now more than 50 per cent of the world's population is in social media, a third of them on Facebook alone, and despite a slew of scandals about data breaches and meddling in election results, at scale it would seem that Facebook only continues to grow and get stronger.

The future of any communication strategy, either one-to-one (as in salespeople to their clients) or one-to-many (such as marketing departments talking to industries, sectors or companies), must, must, MUST include social media as a major part of it. Irrespective of the possibility that technology adds these exciting extra dimensions to our social media interactions, people are still signing up to join this movement at a staggering rate: five new profiles are created every single second – that's 18,000 per hour or 432,000 every day.

Yes, that's exponential growth and yes, that's just Facebook. Add LinkedIn, Snapchat, Instagram, WhatsApp and you'll get some idea. Now consider that WeChat (the Chinese social network) has much broader functionality than Facebook and is growing even faster.

So, you should be thinking about how social media can be an integral part of YOUR Smarketing roll-out – perhaps a single unifying technology for how the teams listen and interact with each other and with your clients.

The changing face of interruption marketing and advertising

In this book we have talked about the changing way that marketers and salespeople reach out and contact potential buyers. In the old days, before the internet, things were pretty straightforward; the only way to get hold of new customers was to tell them about your product or service. You did this by either calling them up or advertising. In both cases you interrupted what they were doing to tell them.

Are we moving to an ad-free world?

There you are watching a football match and the game is interrupted by an advert, or you go to a website and there is a pop-up. In fact, I think all pop-ups are now called annoying pop-ups. Often these are totally unrelated to anything you want or possibly need. The modern buyer has the power of the internet at their fingertips. Any questions can be answered via search engines, so now when you the salesperson contact them it's just downright annoying. In fact, you are probably damaging your brand by doing it.

What about Generation Z?

A student approached me to do an interview for her dissertation; I asked her about the course and she said, 'The course is great but I have people teaching me things that are not relevant anymore'. 'Such as?', I replied. 'Advertising', she said. The course taught her about how to contact people using advertising on digital platforms and she said that she and her generation (she was 22) lived in an ad-free world.

Use of ad blockers

If you look at the annual Mary Meeker study of the internet you will see that annual online advertising growth in the United States is 22 per cent and this is being driven by mobile; in fact desktop advertising dropped slightly in 2017 (Molla, 2017). Year on year, Google ad spend increased by 20 per cent and year on year, Facebook ad spend growth was 62 per cent.

In this same report it shows that ad blocking grows at 30 per cent year on year. Does anybody watch ads on TV anymore as set-top boxes allow us to fast-forward through these intrusive ads? What is the most annoying ad in the world? That five-second ad on YouTube whenever you play a video.

Content marketing benefits and business case

That said, according to Clear Editorial, 88 per cent of B2B companies are using content as a way to promote their products and services (Nick, 2017).

This seems to make sense; as consumers we go online to research products and services we are about to buy. From wasps' nest removal to cars to $200 million computer outsourcing deals we will go online and research the whys and wherefores. If we are going to expend our political capital taking an idea to the board of our company, we will have researched all the options and all the possible questions we might get and we will have done this online.

People only remember you when they see the ad, not because they have short memories but there are so many ads. Ads are often competing with ads. Just watch TV in the United States and there are sponsors and ads everywhere; for me TV there is totally unwatchable. So people remember you as long as you advertise. If you stop advertising, you are out of people's minds.

If we take Stewart Rogers' *Venture Beat* article (Rogers, 2016), content marketing was up 300 per cent but only 5 per cent of it is read. Content marketing is up 300 per cent, but only 5 per cent of it matters.

In our experience, not all content is the same. In many companies we deal with we have seen that content creation is a 'tick box' exercise, where marketing will create content, we guess as part of a personal objective. If it's read, resonates with a client or helps the sales teams get a meeting, nobody seems to care. They have ticked the box.

Which is a pity, as NTT Security have worked out that for every 8.6 blogs they post they get one lead (Passle, nd) and according to Hubspot, companies that publish 16 blog posts get 4.5 times more leads per month (Hubspot, 2018).

In fact, companies such as IBM, American Express and Coca-Cola are finding that not spending on adverting has no impact on revenues. Actually, revenues are going up.

So, the benefits of content marketing are that it:

- creates brand awareness;
- establishes an emotional connection;
- encourages your customer to engage with (maybe ask questions of) your brand;
- educates potential buyers;
- differentiates you from your competition;
- tells stories of successful use cases;
- improves search engine rankings.

Content marketing is hard work as it requires you (or your agency) to write something that is engaging that will be liked and shared on social networks. But one piece of content isn't enough; you need to create a series. For example, our company creates one piece of original content every day. We don't need to advertise and we are able to get the search engine optimization (SEO) we need.

Should marketing and HR merge?

When we started our company one of the earliest pieces of work we did was with the HR (what used to be called personnel) department of a larger accountancy firm in London. We took part in a two-day workshop where we brainstormed the future of the department in terms of recruitment, communicating with the outside world, the future of work, the future of working with millennials and an ageing population as some of the areas.

Does branding sit with HR?

One of the areas we discussed was where does 'brand' sit? The HR department was very clear that 'the brand' sat with them. The argument went like this.

They were involved in recruiting people (or talent as they called it); the touchpoints from the very start of the process to recruit someone were about brand, right to the point where the person was recruited, until the person left. This was all about brand and employee (customer) experience (CX).

We discussed with them that their employees were some of their best brand advocates. IBM use employee advocacy for 'marketing' as well as 'talent acquisition' purposes. When employees love your brand they are passionate about their work and then externalize this passion on social media. This clearly is a way to amplify the message of the organization. This is why HR needs to have clear, strong brand values and needs to take part and have a leadership role in branding.

Is HR responsible for revenue or talent or both?

The challenge is often that HR is seen as a cost centre and is tracking the more natural 'hire to fire' aspects and processes, but uncovering a company's values, and communicating these to the employees, is where HR can rally the employees and add value to the organization.

The challenge is moving away from pamphlets or e-mails, which have been traditional HR methods of communication to employees, towards where employees are embracing new day-to-day actions to get involved and externalize the culture for the good of the organization. Revenue or talent.

This is one area where you definitely need a top-down approach; there have to be key stakeholders that can launch this internally and lead from the front. Traditionally this would be launched at a company meeting, with a back-up of content such as employee videos and infographics that tell and explain the story.

As so often in social programmes, once you have a top-down buy-in, you also need bottom-up (grassroots) buy-in and support. In other words, there needs to be a core of evangelists who own the brand values and start to share content online, as well as best practice with the rest of the employees.

Don't forget employees at the centre as well as locations; in addition, if you have resellers (value-added resellers (VARs)) etc, you should also bring them into the programme. The more people speaking well about your brand the better, for so many reasons.

Blockchain

While Blockchain has been seen as a technology to be used within fintech and supply chain, there is debate that going forward, Blockchain will be used in sales and marketing departments.

Before we go any further, what is Blockchain?

Blockchain was originally developed as the secure basis for the Bitcoin currency. And no doubt you will have seen and heard so much about how Blockchain is going to revolutionize e-commerce and many other sorts of online transactions. You've probably also heard people talk about how it's a transformation that's as important as the internet itself!

So, could this be the case?

Well, yes and no! It's unlikely to be as important as the internet itself, but it's going to be incredibly important in the future of business and here's why.

Every transaction requires some kind of record to make it valid. Imagine ordering something online and not getting any sort of acknowledgement that you'd done so. If the item never arrived you would have no way of proving that you'd paid for it.

In traditional transactions people send receipts and the financial aspect of the transaction is handled by a trusted source – usually the bank. The problem is, though, that you have to trust the banks and all banks take time to process the transaction and charge fees for doing it. It's been very difficult to change this because removing the bank also removes the trust and the surety that all parties are going to get what they expect – payment for goods.

But with Blockchain things work a bit differently. Everyone in the Blockchain network has a copy of the ledger (or transactions) so if one party tries to change their record this will be recorded throughout the network and it makes fraud almost impossible.

This means that the banks are no longer required and with no banks, transactions travel through the network much faster and for zero cost because there are no fees.

What does that mean in real terms? It gives people in the network the opportunity to transact business more quickly, with more security and with no cost; for organizations with very complex supply chains this can be a huge improvement in efficiency.

So how does this impact marketing?

Blockchain in marketing is still (at the time of writing) in its very early days; however, a list of the products that want to be defined as Blockchain marketing products can be found here: http:// bit. ly/2FHtiwo.

Currently, advertising seems to be the first area that is being developed; you will have already read our views that advertising has had its day and consumers of social networks, especially millennials and Generation Z, are not interested.

Where Blockchain can disrupt that industry is where there are 'middle men' and where the buyer of the adverts seems to get opaque measurements, mainly as the market is still controlled by 'old school' advertising and marketing agencies that get a commission and still think that 'eyeballs' is a legitimate measure.

One such article on Blockchain and marketing (Infovore, 2017) quotes that for every $1 of advertising invested the purchaser only gets $0.44 of value.

In addition, one Forrester analyst (Vega, 2011) claims that removing middle men with Blockchain could put another $4 of value back into the system for the buyer of the ads.

There is also a continuing debate about ad fraud and the use of bots and chatbots. A recent article (Slefo, 2016) estimated ad fraud at US $7.2 billion.

Where will this end?

I don't think anybody knows; we look forward to seeing new developments and applications. To quote a recent article from chiefmartec.com (Brinker, 2017):

> In a blockchain world, everything that can be tokenized will be
> tokenized and everything that can be decentralized will be decentralized.
> Which is why there is a good chance that many of the companies on the
> martech landscape list will have a decentralized equivalent in some form
> or fashion.

Sales commission

Anyone who has experience of selling complex, large-scale B2B solutions will know that the rewards can be excellent. Successful salespeople rarely grumble about their remuneration.

Tim recounts the story of when he got a role at a large US software company and was given a set of accounts to 'look after'. Tim is a new business guy, he likes taking an empty territory and turning it into a lush area that can feed not just him and his family, but also a team of farmers, and this wasn't that.

As he was given the accounts he was told, 'something seems wrong, but we are not sure what it is'. So he visited the customer and it was clear that what they had been sold and what they thought they had bought were two very different things. The value proposition was and should have been sold to big companies and this was a mid-market company.

When he got back to the office, he got a copy of the approvals and found out they had all been forged. He wrote a report and his conclusion was 'to apologize and give the customer their money back'. Of course, the supplier didn't do this and a fractious relationship carried on for another two years until the client cancelled.

What about the salesperson who originally sold it? They were posting photos on social media about their yacht near Barbados. In fact, customer after customer can tell you about signing for something only for the salesperson to disappear.

Now this isn't about hunters vs farmers. But in 2018, selling something and disappearing does not fit most buyers' idea of a great customer experience. Surely if you sell something you need to have some 'skin in the game' on the success of the project?

Compensation does drive behaviour

We're not advocating a pay cut. Salespeople take a big risk and they are the engine room to drive the future cashflow of the company, but they need to be thinking 'long-term relationship' rather than 'one-night stand' in any risk and reward relationship. There is of course a risk for the sales team if they are being paid on customer success, which is that they are reliant on other people, people who may not be as bothered or concerned as the salesperson (who is incentivized to be so). Perhaps this is a sacrifice worth making to support a customer's long-term business?

So how should salespeople be paid? Well, that will be, as we discussed earlier, a matter for your organization, but a failure to retain good salespeople may well cause more problems than it solves.

To sum up

Remember that Smarketing is not the destination; it is part of the journey. In the merged world of sales and marketing (Smarketing), one such department within an organization at the mercy of both changes in customer behaviour and the transformational effects of technology and the advances it brings, there will never be true stability. Everything will be subject to change.

The nature of AI, social media, team structures, compensation, regulations, Blockchain and a million other variables means that agility in the deployment of Smarketing will be crucial to its success.

The truth of the matter is, though, that there is no viable alternative to Smarketing as organizations become ever more connected with their customers (and ever more connected within themselves), joining the dots, for better or worse, making it not just easier but inevitable.

As marketing's role moves closer to sales the KPIs will cease to be measured as likes, views and clicks and start to be measured as revenue or profit; at this point all the talk about campaigns, pipelines and funnels crystalize into what really matters.

As marketing drives interest and leads, sales drives revenue and the customer drives everything. The customer is empowered, the customer is available (if you know how to get to them) and the customer is the one we're asking to spend their money.

Welcome to Smarketing, welcome to the future.

Questions to ask yourself

1 Write a letter to your future self that you will open in nine months. In this letter, itemize what you will achieve in your Smarketing programme, visualize where you want to be in nine months and write it down.

2 Write on a sheet of paper your single next action and tweet us, either as a selfie or take a photograph of the sheet – @timothy_ hughes @agsocialmedia and @HugoW_Oracle.

3 If there are other people in your organization that are part of this project, then please recommend they buy a copy of the book and then create a support group. If you don't have a support group, contact us and we will put you in touch with other readers around the world. We are creating a global Smarketing community, to support each other and share best practice.

4 Within your support group have a call every six to eight weeks to share experiences and agree next actions. What can you learn from each other, regardless of business or industry?

5 Please write, blog and share your experiences so that everybody around the world can learn from your experiences. Please help us change the world to a Smarketing world!

References

Brinker, S (2017) The Blockchain marketing technology landscape 2017, *Chiefmartec*. Available at: https://chiefmartec.com/2017/09/blockchain-marketing-technology-landscape-2017/Dscmailtest (2010) [Last accessed 20 June 2018]

Hubspot (2018) The ultimate list of marketing statistics for 2018. Available at: https://www.hubspot.com/marketing-statistics [Last accessed 20 June 2018]

Infovore (2017) Making a change with Blockchain: Revolutionizing the advertising and publishing industry, *Busy*. Available at: http://bit.ly/2KxGG9V [Last accessed 20 June 2018]

Molla, R (2017) Mary Meeker's 2017 internet trends report: All the slides, plus analysis. *Recode*. Available at: https://www.recode.net/2017/5/31/15693686/mary-meeker-kleiner-perkins-kpcb-slides-internet-trends-code-2017 [Last accessed 25 May 2018]

Nick (2017) The content marketing stats every business needs to know, *Clear Editorial Be Contented*. Available at: http://www.cleareditorial.co.uk/content-marketing-stats/ [Last accessed 25 May 2018]

Passle (nd) NTT security. Available at: https://home.passle.net/case-studies/ntt/ [Last accessed 20 June 2018]

Rogers, S (2016) Content marketing is up 300%, but only 5% of it matters. *VentureBear*. Available at: https://www.recode.net/2017/5/31/15693686/mary-meeker-kleiner-perkins-kpcb-slides-internet-trends-code-2017 via @VentureBeat [Last accessed 25 May 2018]

Slefo, G (2016) Ad fraud will cost $7.2 billion in 2016, up nearly $1 billion from 2015, *Adage*. Available at: http://adage.com/article/digital/ana-report-7-2-billion-lost-ad-fraud-2015/302201/ [Last accessed 25 May 2018]

Vega, T (2011) Cutting out middleman to sell small ads online, *New York Times*. Available at: https://www.cnbc.com/id/41828232 [Last accessed 25 May 2018]

YouTube (2010) Minority Report advertising VBR. Available at: https://youtu.be/uiDMlFycNrw [Last accessed 20 June 2018]

INDEX

Note: Page numbers in *italics* indicate Figures or Tables.